"Weary mamas, gather round: Your manifesto for contentment is here. Kate is refreshingly honest, abundantly kind, and compassionately unapologetic. This book is like a yoga session for your heart."

Kendra Adachi, *New York Times* bestselling author of *The Lazy Genius Way,* *The Lazy Genius Kitchen,* and *The PLAN*

"In an era of picture-perfect parenting and endless life hacks, Kate reminds us that contentment isn't another impossible goal. With refreshing honesty, she shows us it's already nestled in our perfectly imperfect daily moments."

Myquillyn Smith, *New York Times* bestselling author of *Welcome Home*

"It takes courage to admit that you feel disappointed by a life that is, on paper, pretty great. Kate does that with humility, solidarity, and one story about Disney World that will make every one of your family vacations seem like paradise by comparison. This book is a breath of fresh air."

Elizabeth Passarella, author of *Good Apple* and *It Was an Ugly Couch Anyway*

"A straightforward approach to adjusting your mindset is what this book is all about. Instead of focusing on what's lacking or what could be better, it encourages a shift toward appreciating your current circumstances. It provides a useful perspective, and it empowers you to cultivate happiness from within, fostering peace and fulfillment in every area of your life."

Myriam Sandler, creator of Mothercould, author of *Playful by Design*

"This is the ultimate playbook for those stuck in the comparison trap. Kate shares practical tips, inspiring stories, and so much wisdom based on personal and shared experiences. Kate is the best friend and big sister we all need guiding us through this messy and beautiful life."

Kelly Stumpe, founder and CEO of The Car Mom, cohost of *The Carpool Podcast*

**I JUST WISH
I HAD A
BIGGER
KITCHEN**

I JUST WISH I HAD A BIGGER KITCHEN

AND OTHER LIES I THINK WILL MAKE ME HAPPY

Kate Strickler

a division of Baker Publishing Group
Minneapolis, Minnesota

© 2025 by Naptime Kitchen, LLC

Published by Bethany House Publishers
Minneapolis, Minnesota
BethanyHouse.com

Bethany House Publishers is a division of
Baker Publishing Group, Grand Rapids, Michigan

Printed in the United States of America

All rights reserved. No part of this publication may be reproduced, stored in a retrieval system, or transmitted in any form or by any means—for example, electronic, photocopy, recording—without the prior written permission of the publisher. The only exception is brief quotations in printed reviews.

Library of Congress Cataloging-in-Publication Data
Names: Strickler, Kate, author.
Title: I just wish I had a bigger kitchen : and other lies I think will make me happy / Kate Strickler.
Description: Minneapolis, Minnesota : Bethany House, [2025] | Includes bibliographical references.
Identifiers: LCCN 2024045343 | ISBN 9780764243783 (cloth) | ISBN 9781493449644 (ebook)
Subjects: LCSH: Happiness—Religious aspects—Christianity. | Christian life.
Classification: LCC BV4647.J68 S78 2025 | DDC 248.8/43—dc23/eng/20241213
LC record available at https://lccn.loc.gov/2024045343

Cover design by Faceout Studio, Spencer Fuller

The Four Loves by C.S. Lewis copyright ©1960 C.S. Lewis Pte. Ltd.
A Grief Observed by C.S. Lewis copyright ©1961 C.S. Lewis Pte. Ltd.
God in the Dock by C.S. Lewis copyright ©1970 C.S. Lewis Pte. Ltd.
Extracts reprinted by permission.

"The Summer Day" by Mary Oliver
Reprinted by the permission of The Charlotte Sheedy Literary Agency as agent for the author. Copyright © 1990, 2006, 2008, 2017 by Mary Oliver with permission of Bill Reichblum

The Proprietor is represented by Alive Literary Agency, AliveLiterary.com.

Baker Publishing Group publications use paper produced from sustainable forestry practices and postconsumer waste whenever possible.

25 26 27 28 29 30 31   7 6 5 4 3 2 1

For Nate,
John Robert,
Scout,
Millie,
and Alberta

Contents

Introduction 11

1. I Just Wish I Had a Bigger Kitchen 19
2. I Just Wish I Was a Better Mom 34
3. I Just Wish I Had a Better Husband 53
4. I Just Wish I Had More Friends 73
5. I Just Wish I Looked Better 88
6. I Just Wish I Had More Money 103
7. I Just Wish I Had More Time 117
8. I Just Wish I Had Control 132
9. I Just Wish My Life Looked More Like Hers 146
10. I Just Wish That Had Gone Better 157
11. A Life You Love 174

Notes 179
Acknowledgments 183

Introduction

> You can go to hell without moving an inch, just focus on what you lack.
>
> You can taste heaven without leaving earth, just rejoice in what you have.
>
> —James Clear

> Folks are usually about as happy as they make up their minds to be.
>
> —Widely attributed to Abraham Lincoln[1]

I have this vivid memory from a few years back. It was a Saturday morning, I had gotten to sleep in a bit, Nate had taken the kids to Dunkin' Donuts and brought me back a hot coffee with cream in it, and we had no set plans for the day. I changed my bedsheets (I relish in fresh sheets, so this is a chore I don't mind doing), tidied up the kitchen, and sat on the back porch while the kids played in the yard. There was a general sense of contentment around the entire morning. I had a home I loved, a family, a hot coffee, and come evening I would be slipping into fresh bedsheets. I had it all.

And then, I opened Instagram.

Introduction

The first photo that came on my screen was of a lifestyle blogger sitting on her own porch (much nicer than mine), wearing the cutest outfit to garden in (I was in an old T-shirt and pair of running shorts). I clicked to her story bubble to find a photo of her coffee cup on her pristine Carrara marble island, followed by her children playing in the sweetest little outfits. I looked into my own yard, where my children looked like feral cats in mismatched pajamas, almost all of them in hand-me-down crocs. Photo after photo showed a life just one step nicer than my own. And that's when the spiral started.

Her porch is larger than mine. Her clothes are nicer than mine. Heck, her children's clothes are nicer than my clothes. Her kitchen is always so clean and beautiful.

Her life is just a little bit better than mine.

I bet she is just a little bit happier as well.

And just like that, my perfect little Saturday morning was robbed from me. And it only took forty-five seconds and the quick tap of an app.

I know this sounds dramatic, but I am sad to say it's the reality of how I've spent so many of my days. I'll be feeling good about myself, and one photo can completely knock me over. Everything I thought was enough is no longer so. I see someone with a standard of living slightly ahead of my own, with an appearance of being able to afford more than I can or travel more than I can, and I get jealous. I believe they are happier. I want the giant kitchen or the lake house. I would even settle for the cute gardening outfit.

But then I keep scrolling. There's been a horrific earthquake in Haiti. Their houses have little to no infrastructure, and the entire country is in shambles. I see photos of children who look like skeletons and a cry for people to donate so they can get clean water.

And just like that my balloon is smacked into the air again. I am the luckiest woman in the world! I have a house with four walls. I have clean water. My children are fed. I live like a queen. I don't need a cute gardening outfit when these people need water. I abandon my Amazon search for new gardening clogs and donate money to the Red Cross.

You see a tragedy, and it completely shifts your perspective. You no longer loathe your body when your close friend finds out she has cancer; you're just grateful to be healthy. You hug your own children extra tight when you read about another shooting, so grateful they made it home that day. Seeing lack and loss in others puts your own abundance on full display.

And this is how we live, floating in a sea of people, bobbing up and down, depending on who we are around.

I know deep down that if I were given the opportunity to trade places at random with someone else in the world, the answer would be *no* every single time. It's too big of a gamble. Over half the world lives in poverty. I am in the top few percent . . . why would I ever risk that? I can even take it a step further and ask if I would want to trade places with any of those top 1 percent, and the answer is still *no*. My life is too specific and precious to trade for another. But if it's so specific and precious, why do I so often find myself wishing for more?

This was the tension I lived in for years—knowing my life was a gift, yet also constantly struggling and comparing it to others. I confused minor inconveniences with calamity and wants with needs. I looked to the left and right, gauging my joy by how well my life stacked up to others. I had such an incredible life, yet I would still go to bed discontent. Sure, there were short Band-Aid fixes that would work for a while. I would get off social media for a bit or have something amazing happening in my own life, but I knew I wanted something more permanent. As a Christian, I knew that deep peace and contentment were found in Jesus, but I also saw myself and so many others struggling with how this played out in the day to day. I craved action steps. I wanted someone to tell me what I could do when my mind was in a mental hole, someone to take the shovel I was digging deeper and deeper with and hand me a ladder to climb out. If this struggle was a sickness, I would never want to fight it without prayer, but I would also not turn away the medications the doctor prescribed. I needed both, working together, to bring healing.

For the better part of the last decade, I have run an Instagram account and blog called Naptime Kitchen, where I post everything from kitchen tips and recipes to thoughts on motherhood and how to get rid of pinworms. The content really runs the gamut, and for that reason, it has allowed me to meet tons of women in different life phases. Some are young moms looking for potty training tips, some are fresh out of college looking for easy recipes, and others are empty nesters reliving those crazy toddler years through my stories. I have had the privilege of understanding the tension between a life you are grateful for and a life you are discontent with on a larger scale. I have read thousands upon thousands of comments and messages from women also caught in this comparison trap. Many are living lives very similar to my own, struggling with a sneaky desire for a life ever so slightly better than the one they have. In all the effort to try to keep up, they are exhausted and desperate for more normalcy online. They want to see messy living rooms and cluttered kitchen counters. They crave unfiltered faces and unfinished spaces.

During my journey to enjoy the life I have, Nate and I watched the movie *Free Solo* with our kids. Free solo climbing is a form of rock climbing where the climbers do not use any ropes or harnesses. The movie follows Alex Honnold, who, at the age of thirty-one, completed the first free solo climb of El Capitan, a vertical rock formation in Yosemite National Park that is three thousand feet from base to summit (if you need a reference, that's over twice the height of the Empire State Building). If Alex were to have fallen, that would have been it for him. No ropes or harness to catch him, just a long fall to his death. He trained with safety ropes to catch him but with the mindset that his life depended on getting it right, because if he was going to climb without ropes, his life would literally depend on it. But the climb was worth it to him; it was worth risking his whole life for.

It wasn't just the physical challenge that drew Alex in. It was also the process: the grace and athleticism that making the climb required, the mental toughness to not only memorize what would work best but also keep trying each time he failed during practice, the beauty of the rhythm he experienced as he moved his hands and legs to the next hold or ledge, the connection and oneness he felt between the rock and his body. For him, there was a physical element as well as a spiritual component. An element of conquest ("I will risk my life to get to the top") and an element of love ("I've never felt more alive than when I'm climbing"). Just because it was hard didn't mean it couldn't also be fun. And each time he failed, it made him all the more hungry to succeed, to figure out what he had done wrong, and to learn from it for next time.

As we watched, I was struck by the parallels I saw between Alex and what I wanted for my own life. For Alex, climbing the mountain was the challenge, but the mountain also provided the substance (the crevices and footholds) for him to hold on to. The more he studied the mountain, the better he climbed. The more he studied the mountain, the more he loved it. I saw my own life taking on this metaphor: Life can feel like climbing a mountain, but it also provides the very substance (people, experiences, mindsets, and faith) to enjoy the climb.

As he trained, Alex made mistakes; he would climb one way only to realize that, if he stayed on his current path, he'd never reach the top. So, he'd backtrack and try a new path. I would likely make mistakes and have to backtrack to the beginning, renaming what mattered to me or figuring out a better way to get where I wanted to go. Sometimes Alex simply got stuck and had to hang on for a bit until he could make a new plan. Likewise, I would get stuck and have to sit and remember the right way to proceed or come up with a new plan entirely. But as I watched Alex do this impossibly hard thing—and love not just the end result but also the process of getting there—I wanted it for myself. I wanted to feel the grit of a hard-earned, ragged and worn, well-loved life.

And so, I started making small mindset shifts and practical applications in my life to fight back every time I caught myself comparing or feeling discontent. Those shifts became my footholds as I climbed. New attitudes slowly began to take root, blooming into a life I wouldn't trade for the world.

In the writing process, I confessed to my book agent, Lisa, that it seemed foolish for someone like me to write a book on the topic of loving one's life. I grew up in a loving household, went to a great college, married an attorney, have four amazing kids, and own a home. My life has had very little hardship. Lisa kindly looked at me from across the table and said, "And yet, you still struggle to love your life." She's right. And my guess is that many of you have walked a similar path to mine. Our needs are met, our children are fed, we fall asleep in warm, cozy beds, and yet we still compare our lives to others' and wish for more.

One sneaky sentence I see playing out in the lives of so many women I love, as well as in my own life, begins with three simple words: "I just wish . . ." It's subtle. You're not looking for a total life overhaul. Most things are totally fine. You just wish your house was a little larger, your bank account a little fatter, your thighs a little slimmer. If your kids were just a bit more well-behaved or your spouse a bit more thoughtful, then . . . then life would be perfect. I know this well because it's a phrase I have used all too often myself. Unfortunately, what I've found over time is that while it's not monumental, these little bits of discontentment can eat away at me over time, causing me to miss out on the sweetness of everyday life right in front of me, the ability to "taste heaven" as James Clear writes. So many times I have wanted to shake a friend and yell, "Look at how incredible your life is—you are wishing it away!" Through this writing, I have realized how often I needed someone to grab my own shoulders, look me in the eyes, and say those words right back to me.

Some of you who pick up this book are going through something legitimately horrible. There might be pain and wounds that require much more care than anything I could write on these pages. You might have a child in the hospital or a cancer diagnosis or be in a financial crisis. Much of what I write likely will not meet you where you are. If I were you, I would feel legitimate anger over someone like me complaining when life is seemingly perfect. But I think that's the issue: So many like me are actually living pretty wonderful lives, if we would open our eyes to see it.

This book is not a memoir but rather a working journal. It contains stories from my own life and practices that have helped me to climb the mountain of loving my life and keep from falling. I do not write as an expert but rather like an alcoholic would write about alcoholism. I have experienced the struggle; I know discontentment and fighting for joy firsthand.

And that's why I wrote this book. Because we all need this reminder. I know it's true, because I've met you in my DMs, on the playground, in the carpool line, and at the dinner table. Women fighting quiet battles of comparison and discontentment that are crushing their happiness and leaving them questioning who they are. Women who go to bed at night feeling overwhelmed by their calendar and underwhelmed by their everyday life, "just wishing" for something more, something different.

And yet. You know you already have enough. So how do you move forward?

Like me, you want to stop waiting for the bigger kitchen, the smaller dress size, and the better-behaved kids before deciding to embrace the climb up your own metaphorical mountain. It's possible, and I know it's possible because I've seen it happen in my own life.

 This book tackles the ten biggest "I just wish" statements I have found women like you and me whispering over the dinner table to our girlfriends or perhaps whispering only to ourselves. I've struggled with all ten of them, and I know how they can each steal my contentment in sneaky ways. I'll share my stories, but I won't leave you empty-handed. At the end of each chapter, I'll give you practical steps that are helping me, plus a mindset shift to drive the point home. I have written the mindset shift in the first person, as a way for you to see yourself in it, almost like a daily affirmation. They are short sayings I have not mastered but deeply need—sayings I am preaching to my own heart. If you, like me, want to love the life right in front of you more, I hope this book helps you get there, one small shift at a time.

CHAPTER
1

I Just Wish I Had a Bigger Kitchen

> There is the great lesson of "Beauty and the Beast"; that a thing must be loved *before* it is lovable.
> —G. K. Chesterton, *Orthodoxy*

Over the last ten years, Nate and I have lived in three homes. Our first home was a duplex in Durham, North Carolina, on this tiny little hidden street right near Duke's campus. We knew the owner, and with a verbal contract to care for all the lawns on the entire street, we lived in a two-bedroom, two-bathroom apartment for $500 a month. It was a steal! We could walk to Duke's campus and Dunkin' Donuts, and nearby there was a super nice apartment with a pool I would sneak into in the summer (I learned if you walked straight in with lots of confidence no one would dare question you). The weekends required a lot of manual labor, but otherwise it was awesome. Nate was in charge of the push mower, I was on the rider, and we tag teamed the weeding. The only downside was in the fall, when I kid you not, I would have a full breakdown when we had to rake and blow fifteen yards' worth of leaves. I have a vivid memory of me crying in the street, blower in hand, attempting to subdue the leaves into a pile. Needless to say it was not working.

Our kitchen in that first home had linoleum floors, plastic countertops, and enough grease in the vent above the stove to fry a Thanksgiving turkey. Before we moved in, Nate and some friends went in and attempted to clean the place as best they could. We didn't live together before getting married, so this would be the first place that we shared an address. Our friend Mason rented a carpet steamer, John Mark and Kelby set to work on the greasy stove with a can of Coca-Cola, and Nate did his best to try to make the little duplex feel like a special first home for us. Once we moved in, I painted the kitchen a bright and happy robin's-egg blue and stocked it with all of my new wedding registry items. It was old and a bit dingy, but it was all mine.

For two and a half years, that little duplex was home, and it was in that outdated linoleum kitchen that I first started to take pictures of the food I was making and post about it. It's also where we brought our firstborn, John Robert, home from the hospital, and I learned the valuable lesson to prep the food before the witching hour. He would nap twice a day, and during that time, I would try out new recipes, scouring the internet for "cheap but fancy" fare. I fell in love with butter and garlic, perfecting the panini (a.k.a. a fancy grilled cheese), and making twenty variations of cowboy caviar. We were less than a mile from Kroger, and I would go multiple times a week, shopping what was on sale or grabbing a specific ingredient for a recipe I was dying to try. I remember making risotto for the first time on an extremely cold day in February. We were watching the news and seeing the absolute mess of cars on I-40; so many people were stuck trying to get home. And there we were, snowed in, with hot risotto and a bottle of Trader Joe's Two Buck Chuck. We felt like millionaires. Eventually, we were forced to move out when a large developer bought the whole block to tear down all those tiny duplexes for a new, shiny apartment building. Strickler Lawn Services would no longer be needed.

From there we found a rental house on Cornwallis Road in Durham. It was a three-bedroom and had a kitchen that fed into a large living room complete with dining area and laundry room (a whole room for laundry!). The floors were now hardwood instead of carpet, and we had a fenced-in backyard. It was fourteen hundred square feet and felt like an absolute mansion. My parents bought us a picnic table for Christmas, and I remember many nights sitting outside on the back patio eating dinner. This house was located on a busy road, so my dad built a tiny wooden gate that allowed us to lock John Robert in on that front porch to keep him contained. Every single afternoon we would sit on this porch and wait for the school buses to start passing by. I would usually hear one before it came into view and would begin chanting, "Bus . . . Bus . . . Bus," getting louder and the words coming more quickly like the theme song of Jaws. As it passed we would both cheer and clap, and then we would wait for the next one. John Robert enjoyed this, and I was so thankful for an easy activity to help pass the time as we waited for Nate to get home.

Once Nate finished law school we moved to Charleston, South Carolina, for his first job as an attorney. John Robert was two, Scout was six months, and I was desperate to be closer to family. We bought a home in West Ashley with the nicest kitchen we had ever experienced. The countertops were granite, the cabinets white with soft-close hinges, and the stove was gas (A gas stove! Just like the professional chefs I watched on TV!). I was so excited to get into the space. Nate's firm had paid for both packers and movers, and the day the moving truck arrived at the new house, both of my mom's sisters were there ready to help us move in. My aunts unpacked my entire kitchen for me, putting things away as best they could and assuring me I could move anything that wasn't where I wanted. They could have put my plates in the drawer underneath the stove for all I cared; I was overwhelmed and grateful for the help.

It's been six years in that same kitchen, and while I have certainly moved some things around, it has essentially stayed the same. And while I do love it, it is not large enough to hold all of my cooking tools. My salad bowls are in a cabinet in the living room, all the foil and extra Tupperware are in a cabinet in the laundry room, and my food processor is down the hallway in a cabinet. While I know where each item is, were someone to go looking for the Instant Pot, it would likely take them hours to locate it. It's comical, really. Aside from the bedrooms, I think there is at least one kitchen item in every single closet in the entire house.

As our family has grown, we have maxed out every square inch of this house. We put on an addition and reworked bedrooms. I have spent countless hours thinking through the best function for each and every cabinet.

Here's a secret: I believe deeply in helping people love the homes they are already in. In enjoying their space and not pining for more. In having that space work and function for them. And yet, I still wonder if my life would really be more enjoyable if I just had a bigger kitchen.

There's a quote hanging on our wall with lyrics from the chorus of Doug Stone's song "Little Houses" all about how small homes are the places where love thrives.

When I see that quote hanging on our wall, I would now say that there are much larger things at play to make our family close than the size of our walls. But for years those words were the balm I needed to feel like the space we had was great. The quote was a way for me to justify our tiny quarters, a way to quell my envy toward those with homes larger and more aesthetically pleasing than mine.

Maybe you have felt this way too, and I want you to know I don't think wanting a bigger kitchen is silly or superficial. Most of us want many of the things I will write about in this book—a thriving marriage, more money, a tighter friend group, etc. But for many of us, the kitchen stands for the comfort, beauty, and contentment we all desire. Social media shows us beautiful, sparkling kitchens with happy kids standing at the counter making homemade cookies with Mom. This whole thing about the kitchen matters, because it's one of the things that can stand for so much more than it really is. It's seen as the "center of the home," the heartbeat of the family, the communal space where everything from homework to meal-prepping happens. Somehow, a beautiful kitchen has come to stand for a beautiful home, beautifully plated dinners, beautifully planned parties, a beautiful family, and a perfectly beautiful life. A spacious kitchen is not going to solve all of life's problems, but when it's 5 p.m. and the kids are screaming at your feet and you're just trying to get dinner made and on the table, that extra space sure does feel like it would make life easier.

    I have always been fascinated with how spaces function. I love design and beauty, but functionality is my sweet spot. While I enjoy any HGTV show, *Tiny House, Big Living* is my favorite. Seeing how they get the most use out of such a small space is extremely satisfying to watch. Last summer I bought a new interior design book filled with page after page of the most gorgeous homes you could imagine. I bought the book to get inspired beyond the basic function of our home. I wanted to see how the designer chose to decorate. When I opened its pages, I saw gorgeous houses with custom drapes and cabinets, spacious kitchens, and entire guest suites. Strangely, I didn't find myself comparing my own home; I felt separated from the designer's work. She is a skilled interior designer; her clients have thousands, if not hundreds of thousands, of dollars to put into their summer lake homes. I could admire the pages, knowing this designer was showcasing what she does best in homes that were immaculate. These homes were larger than mine with larger budgets than mine. Opening a book made for the purpose of interior design felt like stepping into a story. It's lovely, but it's also not my life. It's too far out of reach to compare, and for this reason, I was able to enjoy it.

Somehow, that separation does not translate to life online. Perhaps it's the proximity of photos of people I do know bumped up so closely to people I do not know. My brain starts to get jumbled and confused. I don't remember having these feelings when watching MTV *Cribs*. Sure, Busta Rhymes has a hot tub in his kitchen, but he's Busta Rhymes! Once the era of MTV *Cribs* ended, we had reality TV like *Keeping Up with the Kardashians*, but I still wasn't silly enough to actually compare myself. I am a Strickler; she is a Kardashian. We are not the same.

There used to be a section in *US Weekly Magazine* entitled "Stars! They're Just Like Us!" showing famous people doing "normal people things." Taylor Swift grocery shops, just like me! Mark Zuckerberg walks his dog, just like me! Beyoncé takes her kids to the movies, just like me! (I cannot confirm if the entire movie theater was cleared out and this was a private showing, but in that moment, Beyoncé felt normal.) And that's what we love about it. These people that have felt so far beyond us appear normal, even if only for a brief paparazzi shot.

Social media tends to do the opposite. It takes fairly normal people and catapults them to the strange realm of quasi famous. My mind struggles here. It's easy for me to know I am never going to have the life of Julia Roberts. But what about this other mom of four out in Colorado? We seem similar enough, but her house is three times the size of mine and her counters are spotless. To be fair, this isn't really a social media issue, it's a me issue. I just think social media exacerbates it. It opens me up to hundreds, if not thousands, of new people to keep up with, new homes to get a peek inside. This was not something my grandmother dealt with. She likely saw the homes of close friends, and she would have seen homes of acquaintances even less often. I, on the other hand, see the homes of complete strangers on a daily basis.

Space is really very relative when you think about it, and it usually is only part of the equation. It's space plus location that gets you to cost. A three-thousand-square-foot house outside Charlotte, North Carolina, costs less than a thousand-square-foot apartment in New York City. There are people living in rural South Carolina who own land the size of Central Park, and there are people in Montana whose land is larger than the state of Delaware.

So while space has a lot to do with wealth, I do think it is something entirely different. Some people will sacrifice space for location, and others are going to sacrifice location for space. For many (myself included), you move into a home thinking you'll move out in a few years, but then you fall in love with your neighbors and can't imagine leaving, or the interest rates get so high you're stuck. So, you rearrange and add on and vow to be a minimalist to make it all work. Space is also very relative to who you live around. My friend Lindsey lives in Queens with her family of four in a sixteen-hundred-square-foot apartment. The living room is the kitchen which is the family room. But it's got two bedrooms! In Queens, that's a luxury. In Queens, Lindsey has a ton of space. However, if you put Lindsey's family in that same apartment in Charleston, people would say they were too crowded and should move.

For me, space has always been deeply tied to my anxiety. When I am anxious, I crave more space as an escape. I want clear counters and minimal visual clutter. My body is having trouble breathing and thinks that what it needs is literally more room to breathe. Paradoxically, when I am anxious, I do not want to be alone.

The house I grew up in was large, and when I was in sixth grade we did a big addition on one side, essentially giving my parents their own wing of the house. As a parent, I absolutely get this. They wanted some space, a place to retreat to at the end of long days with four children. This renovation also meant I got my own bedroom and would no longer have to share with my sister. As nice as it was to have my own bedroom, I was easily scared and wished my parents' bedroom was closer. They were on the other side of the house, and I was very skeptical they would be able to hear my screams should kidnappers come to take me.

As nice as that renovation was, I remember on multiple occasions missing the smaller space we once shared. I missed sharing a sink with Anna to brush our teeth and sneaking into Albert's room when I was scared. In college, I stayed with my friend Courtney and noticed that all the bedrooms were on the second floor of the house, snug and close together. I loved how safe and cozy it felt. What's funny is that Courtney definitely wished for a larger house; where I saw closeness she saw crowdedness.

When we first moved to Charleston and became a part of a church, I remember getting invited to an Easter egg hunt with a bunch of ladies from the church. I was new and therefore didn't know many people, but I was told we were going to "Meg's house on James Island" and given the address. Meg was a mom of four, and from all I could see on the outside she was a very cool, well-known woman in the church. I do not know what I was expecting when I got to the house, but this was not it. Meg was in cutoff jean shorts and a T-shirt. There were kids everywhere using every single outdoor toy she had. When I went inside, Meg's house was floor-to-ceiling bursting with life and chaos. There was an entire gallery wall of her kids' artwork in mismatched frames that poured down the hallways and into the family room. The kids' rooms were not particularly tidy or themed in any way. There were posters and blankets and stuffed animals each representing what that child loved. But the kitchen is what struck me the most. Meg had a tiny kitchen. The cabinets were filled to the brim, the fridge was a standard side by side, and there was barely enough counter space to make dinner, let alone space for an island and barstools. This was not the quintessential hosting house you see in the magazines.

Around lunchtime, Meg brought out a Chick-fil-A nugget platter for the kids, and then, from her tiny little kitchen, she prepared one of the best salads I have ever eaten. Lettuce reached the brim of the giant wooden bowl; there were pistachios and segmented oranges bursting with flavor. There was fresh avocado and the creamiest, dreamiest dressing I have ever tasted. It was heaven. Other friends had brought their own additions to the meal, but all I really remember was that salad.

I left Meg's house with a new resolve to love my home and make it my own. To fill the walls with artwork and allow the kids the freedom to make their rooms whatever they wanted them to be. It's strange how much I wanted my home to feel like Meg's home. It wasn't perfect or neat or tidy, but it was welcoming and warm. It was a place I felt I could exhale and allow my kids to enjoy. It was a feeling—like her entire home was surrounded by some sort of "this is unashamedly who we are" aura. I knew what she had created didn't require a massive renovation or new furniture, but it did require work. She had to take a metaphorical sledgehammer to the standards of what her home was supposed to be and instead lean into what she wanted it to be. This was something I could tell she had done because she was happy to host, not once apologizing for the state of her space. In Meg's eyes her home was not separate from her family but rather a living, working representation of who they were, and she loved inviting people into that. It reminded me of my dad's sister, whom we call Aunt Ellen. When my grandfather passed away, my grandmother slowly got to a place where she couldn't host Christmas morning anymore. During this time, Aunt Ellen's home became the new meeting spot for Christmas morning. It was also during this time that the Freemans were seriously starting to procreate. Each year, there would be more babies and toddlers, slowly wreaking havoc on her home. Despite the onslaught of toddlers, Aunt Ellen was always beaming from ear to ear. I have told her multiple times how welcoming her house is, how cozy and safe it feels. It's not that she doesn't have nice things or lives in disarray, but she seems to regard her stuff lightly. It's like she knows that nothing is so irreplaceable it is worth fussing over (or at least nothing in easy reach of a toddler). She has this ease about her the entire time we are there, encouraging us to sit on the sofa and have some of her famous pimento cheese.

I have seen this same desire in my own parents. When they started having grandkids, they knew they wanted to see them often, so they started to make a home that reflected that desire. They turned one of the bedrooms into a nursery, complete with a crib and changing table. They stocked the house with diapers. They even bought a baby monitor. When the toddlers started potty training, they bought a toddler potty. While their home still has a ton of beautiful things in it, Mom moved her most treasured pieces out of the reach of small hands and cleared the coffee table of breakable items. Their home reflected the season of life they were in and what their desires were, and it worked. Now, on any given day, you can find one of my siblings at my parents' home, the adults conversing in the kitchen while the grandchildren play in the playroom or on the play set my parents installed. All of these homes have something in common to me. They reflected the season of life each person was in and were functioning in a way that best served the people living in them. The space was serving the people who lived there, rather than the people feeling like they needed to serve the space. Meg's kids felt celebrated by those walls filled with their artwork. I felt welcomed into Aunt Ellen's cozy living room. My kids beg to go to Berber and Poppa's house. All of these spaces created feelings we long for: welcoming and belonging.

With this in mind, I started to focus more on how my home functioned than how it looked. I started to ask myself *Is this working well for my family?* instead of *Does this look like the cover of a magazine?* And slowly, as I worked to create a space that was unashamedly ours as opposed to what I thought home was supposed to look like, it became more lovely to me. The more we lived in our home, the more it reflected who we were and what we valued. My home felt like a hunk of wood I was whittling away, carving and scraping what didn't work to make room for what did. The more I shaped it and made it my own, the more I began to love it. Over time, I became convinced that a home has to be loved to feel lovable. A house has to be used to feel like a home.

Years after this initial realization, we had two sets of friends and their kids come and visit us in Charleston. One family stayed at our house, and the other at an Airbnb close by. It was unseasonably warm for November, and we had the most gorgeous day outside. Then the temperature dropped drastically, and by Saturday it was cold and rainy, and our house became the hangout spot for the weekend.

At one point, every single surface had stuff on it. Cups galore, dirty dishes, countless socks missing their owners, shoes on the floor, and dress-up clothes in every room. My small kitchen quickly became Grand Central Station for drinks and pizza and more snacks than any one person could eat. We made margaritas to sip alongside chips and queso. We cooked bacon and eggs for breakfast and threw together peanut butter and jellies for lunch. We used up every single rag wiping up water spills from the kids, and we finally got smart, switching to Solo cups and a black Sharpie to keep the cup usage manageable.

We really could have used more space. In that moment I genuinely wanted a giant countertop with ample barstool seating. I wanted a second floor to banish the rambunctious kids to. I wanted to apologize to my friends for not having more room for them. But the more I look back on that weekend, I've realized the space I had in no way deterred from the richness we felt being together. My home was doing exactly what it was made to do: It was holding people and their mismatched socks and their cups.

It was being dirtied and tidied and dirtied again. In all its imperfections, there it was, doing what it did best: bringing people together, feeding them, and sheltering them (quite literally) from the storm.

As a mom, it's a sweet freedom to suddenly see marks and spills as signs of life instead of annoyances. And when people come to your home, you realize, "I don't need to apologize for these things. I do not live in a museum. I live with five other humans, four of them under the age of nine. There are going to be handprints on the walls and scratches on the floors."

Over the summer, we had a photoshoot at the house to take pictures for my website. There was a professional photographer and a person specifically in charge of lighting. Those two made my kitchen look absolutely dreamy, and I love how the photos turned out. However, the moment they were gone, we took all the hidden things needed for our everyday life back out. The grocery list came back out of the drawer, and kids' cups went back on the counter. The coffee maker was set out along with the blender. Photos and the kids' report cards went back on the fridge. And as much as I loved the clear surfaces we had for the photos, there was something comforting about the items we use so often being put back where they were needed, when all the things that made our kitchen unique to us came back out of hiding. Ironically, the things that I started off saying gave me anxiety also brought comfort, I think because they are the very things that make my home my home. The things that give me belonging.

I still struggle with the size of our home, especially our kitchen. And if I am honest, I think I will always believe it would be easier if we just had a little more space. I am currently learning how to decorate and have a nice home but not allow myself to be consumed by it. I am learning how to have nice things while also having a place where my kids feel free to relax and unwind. I am not sure how this will pan out, and it will likely require a lot of give-and-take on both sides, but I think that's ok. Our home is a tool we are all learning to use. There are ways we need to respect it and ways it's ok for it to get dinged up a bit. Those marks are signs it is doing its job well. The more we use it, the more we love it; it is beautiful because it is used; it is lovely because it is loved.

> **MINDSET SHIFT:** My home is a tool that reflects the season of life I am in; it can create feelings of welcome and belonging no matter the style or size.

·········· MAKING IT PRACTICAL ··········

1. If you struggle with your space, I want you to know that is not silly. Our space has an incredible effect on our lives. It's home, after all. We live and sleep and eat our meals within these walls. Your kids live here and want to have friends over. Also, getting more space doesn't happen overnight. If your space really is feeling overly stimulating or cluttered, consider getting a few large bins and removing as much of the clutter as you can. Leave it in the bins, and only take things out as needed. After six months, see what remains and if you missed any of the items. If not, consider donating.

2. Kelle Hampton (@ETST on Instagram) did an eye-opening activity in 2022 when she went through some of the most beloved movies and TV shows of the last twenty years and specifically looked at their kitchens. In each one, the things you noticed the most were how homey and unique they were. Most were not huge, and none, save for that of Amanda Woods's

pristine California kitchen in *The Holiday*, was especially neat or tidy. But it seems even that was making a point. Amanda Woods's life was falling apart, and despite her clean kitchen and massive home, all she wanted to do was escape. As you watch some of your favorite shows this year, take a look at the kitchens. What stands out most?

3. The kitchen is one area of the home where I really believe you are fully allowed to stretch the boundaries. I keep extra food containers and rarely-used cooking utensils in the laundry room. I know where to find them when I need them, and they aren't taking up my precious kitchen space. Remember, your home is yours to use however you need. The Crock-Pot really can live in the hall closet if there's no cabinet space left.

4. Something I have come to embrace is small corners of my house where everything feels calm and put together. Myquillyn Smith (author of *House Rules*, *The Nesting Place*, and *Cozy Minimalist Home*) calls this "one sane space."[1] For me, that's my bedroom. I make my bed every morning, and I know, at any given time of day, I can walk in there to a made bed and a small leather chair in the corner that looks out the window. When the rest of the house feels chaotic, that's my beloved corner, my one sane space. This week, look around your home and decide what your one sane space could be. If you don't have one, seek to create one! It doesn't have to be large or elaborate—just a corner you can go to when you need a little sanity.

5. It is so easy to get caught up in photos of pristine homes with matching bedding and correlating wallpaper. While those things are wonderful, I challenge you to begin to think of your home less like a photo and more like a tool. As you go about your day, take note of all the many ways you use it in a day. The basket by the front door that is the perfect place to house

keys, the painting in the kitchen that makes you smile, the cutting board and knife always within arm's reach to slice an apple and some cheese. Each and every time you use a part of your home, you are honoring it. You are allowing it to do what it was made to do.

CHAPTER
2

I Just Wish I Was a Better Mom

> You have to do your own growing no matter how tall your grandfather was.
>
> —attributed to Abraham Lincoln

> Yet everybody thinks of changing the world, and nobody thinks of changing himself.
>
> —Leo Tolstoy, *Three Methods of Reform*

I am currently entering a phase of parenting that feels completely foreign and overwhelming to me. My older two are only eight and six, but the emotional roller coasters we ride have already begun. I feel like we're on the smaller rides at the theme park; you know it could be bumpy and twisty, but you're not going fully upside down yet. The full-body harness and 360-degree loops where your stomach drops out and you lose all sense of which way is up will come with the teen years, just you wait.

The hard part is how different these emotions feel from the little years, and how much less control I have in the situation. This isn't tears over a toy or a snack Mom said they couldn't have. No one is dropping to the floor kicking and screaming. But it's also much harder to know what they are actually upset about. Are mood rings accurate? If only.

The other morning, my oldest two were making muffins, and at some point, Scout started to sing an annoying song that bothered John Robert. He asked her to stop. She didn't. He asked again. She persisted. So, naturally, he kicked her. I saw the whole thing and told him he needed to go be in his room for a bit until I came to talk to him. That meant he would not get to be the one to take the muffins out of the oven (a task only he was old enough to do and relished in). I figured this would be much like any other discipline moment. I would go talk to him about how we never use violence against others. He would apologize to his sister for kicking her. She would apologize for not listening to him when he asked her to stop. We would each eat a muffin. Boom. Super Mom doing what she does best over here, keeping everyone together one scuffle at a time.

That is not what happened. When I went into John Robert's room, he was furious to the point of being completely irrational. He would not talk to me, did not want to talk to his sister, and essentially had that wild look in his eye you usually only see in rabid animals. He traipsed away from me while I was midsentence . . . and that was when I yelled. I took him by the arm, walked him back into his room, and told him I would come back in a half hour. Essentially, he was in time-out.

I went back to getting the girls breakfast in the kitchen while, unbeknownst to me, John Robert was in his room packing a bag and writing me a note that read, "You do not need me here. No one will miss me." He was going to run away. All that in the span of one hour, which started with the wholesome, memory-making opportunity of banana muffins.

I am not sure what I should have done. Looking back, I know I shouldn't have yelled, but should I have put him in his room for a half hour? Was there a different or better tactic I could have used? I really tried to listen to why he was upset and enter in. I told his sister in front of him that what she did was wrong as well. I told her that she needed to apologize. I was gentle, but also stern. I felt like I was being the referee everyone needed, and it still all went up in flames. Where did I go wrong?

There are things about the way my mom parented us that were really good and helpful and other things I want to do differently. But in the moment, when the adrenaline kicks in, it is so hard to know what I am doing from a place of wisdom and what I am doing out of spite or anger. What am I doing because I choose to, and what am I doing because that's the only way I have seen it done? I've heard the joke that you should start a savings account now for all the therapy your kids will need when they're older because of the way you parented them; I am beginning to believe it's not a joke.

Dr. Becky Kennedy's online parenting account on Instagram skyrocketed during Covid, and for good reason. She would start her videos with simple role-play. For instance: A mom asking the child to clean the room, the child claiming they had done so, the parent noticing it wasn't clean and then trying to decide how to respond.[1] These videos went viral because the situations felt so familiar, and every parent was desperate for help. She also gave scripts to use with word-for-word ways to dissipate an escalating situation. To the strung-out, exhausted, trapped-at-home mom, these scripts felt like a beacon of hope. They held an "if you do this you won't royally screw up your child" promise we all desired. We were all home with our kids, wanting to know if the way we were handling the situation was the best way. We were looking from left to right, clueless, hoping we were making choices that wouldn't land us with those huge therapy bills years later.

This next phase of parenting feels hard and scary in ways much deeper than the little years. The stakes feel higher. Their memory lasts longer. I could say something that could really hurt them, creating ripples that affect them for years to come.

No pressure, Mom.

Early on in my Instagram career, I had an evening when I made a salmon dish for the kids. I had bought the salmon from the frozen section of Whole Foods and was so pleased with the way I had prepared it: a teriyaki glaze sprinkled with sesame seeds and steamed rice and green beans on the side. I showed the process on my Instagram, including the salmon I had purchased. Within an hour, I had multiple messages telling me I really should be using wild-caught salmon; farm-raised salmon were fed a worse diet and was therefore worse for my kids. Some went so far as to say that salmon was harming my children.

There I was, a young mom with two young kids, being told by strangers on the internet my meal of salmon (salmon, for crying out loud!) was unhealthy. I needed to do my research when it came to feeding my children. I also needed to make sure to give them lots of fruits and veggies, but make them organic. I needed to teach them how to eat what I serve but also not force them to eat—I wouldn't want to create habits that could form an eating disorder down the road. I should let them eat sweets (food freedom!) but not too many (sugar is poison) and watch those snack choices while I was at it. After all, as their parent, I was the person responsible for these decisions. How I fed them mattered, creating ripples that would impact their health for years to come.

No pressure, Mom.

One of my biggest regrets in life is quitting piano lessons. That's dramatic. But I really do wish I could play the piano. I have this dream of me sitting down casually at a friend's house and playing Chopin from memory; my very own party trick. Our house would have a special spot by a window for our piano, and my precious children would be serenaded by their mother before bed. What a Renaissance woman I would be!

I took lessons back in middle school but did not have an ounce of natural knack for the ivory keys. Funny enough, my mom also took piano as a child and had little to no talent (I believe her piano instructor finally told her she really should just quit). I gave it a good year of my life before telling my mom I didn't enjoy piano at all, and she was completely fine with me quitting. I was already playing sports and, being one of four children, I am sure she was a bit relieved to have one less thing to shuttle me to weekly.

What I loved was playing basketball and volleyball. Looking back, I had no future in those sports. I was decent, but you were not looking at a D1 athlete. But that's where my passion was, and so that's what I stuck with. My mom would drive me to weekend volleyball games in the most rural parts of South Carolina, spending her entire Saturday sitting in a giant gymnasium and sleeping in a crappy hotel so I could play in the two-day long tournaments.

Now that I am an adult, I really wish I would have stuck with piano and maybe let go of basketball a bit earlier in life. Piano feels like something I could still enjoy, whereas I rarely pick up a basketball. But hindsight is, as they say, twenty-twenty, and like I said, I really wasn't good at piano. My mom probably knew that I didn't have a future as an athlete, but she was willing to give of her time to let me play because I loved it. After I joined the travel team, I am sure she would have preferred a weekly piano lesson to those two-day volleyball tournaments. But should she have pushed me to stick with piano? Maybe she was so quick to let me quit because she too had a bad experience learning piano. Perhaps had she stuck with it, I would have stuck with it. It's hard to say. Maybe I would have been great and so thankful for her persistence. Maybe I would have done lessons for two more years, barely improving, and still quit, losing two years of both my parents' time and money and having a lot of fights in the process.

Herein lies one of a million small decisions my mom made, each decision creating ripples, shaping me into the person I am today.

No pressure, Mom.

We live in an area where the conversation of where your child will go to middle school feels equivalent to where they will go to college. Nate did not grow up this way. His hometown had one public school, and that's simply where everyone went. Rich, poor, Black, and white were all at the same school. In Charleston, we have zoned public schools and a myriad of charter and magnet schools. Each year, there's a system called "school choice," where you basically put your name into a giant hat along with thousands of other kids and hope your child's name gets pulled for the school you want. It's a total crapshoot. Some schools are great for elementary, but the middle school has a poor reputation. For others it's the opposite. Since we have a child entering fourth grade, the topic of middle school is top of mind for everyone. There's public school, and there's private school. There's charter schools and magnet schools and, heck, even boarding schools. You want them to have a good education. You want them to meet different kinds of people. You don't want to have a forty-five-minute commute. You want them to have friends that carry over from elementary school.

Whether we make the choice or the zoning makes the choice for us, where your child goes to school will affect them, creating ripples that will determine their future.

No pressure, Mom.

"Babies don't keep."

"You only get eighteen years with them."

"You will miss this."

"Cherish every moment."

I know time passes. I know my kids are going to grow older. Their squishy, soft baby feet will turn into smelly teenager feet. They will go from needing me every moment to needing me every so often. And one day, they will move out. Sure, it's absolutely exhausting and demanding, but it won't last forever, so I better cherish every moment. I better soak it all up. Otherwise, I'll regret it for years to come.

No pressure, Mom.

As much as I loathe that last paragraph, it is where my biggest struggles lie. I don't lose sleep over Skittles, much less salmon. I don't really stress about what activities the kids quit and which ones they stick with. I feel confident we will be ok in the quagmire of school decisions. At the end of the day, my biggest fear is regretting not being with them more; I believe those other worries will work out if I am there for them—if I just make sure I am around and present. My biggest struggle is what my role as mom should look like: What things do I give my time to, and what am I ok to miss? What are the nonnegotiables in this role, and what things are specific to our family and my children?

I grew up in a household where my dad worked and my mom was home with their four children. She packed the lunches and carted us to various practices and activities. She managed the household and cooked dinner. I loved all the ways she was present for us growing up and saw her role in our family as something to aspire to. Her job was being our mom; her days were largely dictated by the needs of her four children. *What I didn't realize was that I had formed a framework for what motherhood looked like without really asking if that same framework was best for my own family.*

While I had been running Naptime Kitchen since my firstborn was six months old, I still heavily considered myself a stay-at-home mom because, well, I was. If the kids had a doctor's appointment, I was the one to take them. I did the school pickups and drop-offs and dentist appointments. Anything that happened between the hours of eight and six was my job, because Nate was at the office. And while there were plenty of days it was extremely difficult, I also felt a sense of pride and power for who I was in that role. I was *Mom*. If the kids needed something, I was the primary person they would ask because I was the one with all the answers. Was there an extra bottle of ketchup in the pantry? Did we have more toilet paper? Did we pick up cupcakes for the class party? I had all of those answers; I was lord of the household.

After Nate left his full-time job, he started to take on a lot of the load around the house, and while I was so grateful, I also felt a sense of panic. *Who am I now? Am I a working mom? Do my kids still come to me with their needs?* This all became exacerbated by the fact that our fourth child, Alberta, absolutely favored Nate. If she was sad or tired, she wanted Nate. I believed she loved him more than me because I wasn't around enough.

I decided I would be there in every capacity as Mom but also expand what was happening for Naptime Kitchen. This was bad for two reasons: First, it wasn't sustainable. It left me feeling guilty in both areas and constantly tired. And second, it stunted the ways Nate really could help because I was afraid of losing this part of my identity.

I don't think men struggle with their identity in parenting in nearly the same way that women do. I do not think that Nate felt guilt when he left for work in the morning. He was leaving to go and provide for our family, and that's simply the way it had to happen. I, on the other hand, was afraid that I would look back in twenty years and regret not being home more. I only get them for eighteen years; my babies won't keep. I am not alone in this tension. I know so many mothers who work and feel a level of guilt putting their children in daycare. Likewise, I know so many mothers who are home full-time and feel guilty because they are desperate for time away from their kids.

Interestingly, I found that friends who came from households where the mom worked did not feel the same guilt I was feeling; they had a loving, caring mom who also happened to work. They did not see the roles of *Mom* and *working parent* at odds with one another the way I did. Not to mention the tons of friends whose moms didn't have the luxury to choose whether they worked or not.

I also realized that a lot of friends had husbands who worked from home or had flexible jobs, allowing for more shared responsibilities in the household. They did not hold "motherhood as martyrdom" to the degree that I did. And here is where I discovered a large reason this was so hard for me: I wanted to do it all. To me, being a good mom meant doing it all. Sure, I wished for Nate to be around more, I wished for more help, but I felt a deep sense of pride in all that I did for my family. I did it. Me! And I wanted praise and worship for it. I wanted people to look in and think, *Wow! How does she do it all?* My worth as a mom became attached to what I *did* instead of who I *was*. The funny thing about motherhood, however, is that your kids do grow up. What you do for them does change; you want it to. You want to raise children to become capable adults who no longer need you. We mourn their flying the nest as we train them daily to be able to do just that.

A few months into these motherhood-identity questions I was having, I hung out with my friends Kristen and Lindsay. They each had two children, and it was the first year that both of their children were in school full-time. Both of these moms now had around seven hours a day kid-free. And you know how both felt? Disoriented. Both were asking what they were meant to be doing in this new phase of their lives. Lindsay was thinking of signing up to be a substitute teacher or working with her husband on the administration side of his business. Kristen was volunteering more in her children's classrooms and helping her parents more. Both could feel the shift in their role happening and were left wondering how to fill the time. I have seen this more and more: My friend Ruthie is now working at the front desk of her kids' school; Sarah just applied for an admin job. All are looking for ways to fill a newly given void that school-age children allow, while wondering what their role in this next phase looks like. I realized the identity crisis I was having was one so many women face: Who am I outside of motherhood? I believe this is the same way many men feel when they retire. Who am I outside of my work? The difference is that retirement tends to come around sixty-five, whereas the shift in motherhood roles happens much, much earlier.

I didn't want to view my motherhood journey as some short-term project I needed to suck every ounce of life out of. At this rate, I'll be thirty-eight when all my kids are in school; I'll be fifty when my youngest goes to college. I didn't want to put all my effort and energy into one focus and be left floundering when my kids were no longer home. Despite the onslaught of one-liners and books telling me I need to soak up every moment of this phase, I didn't want to center my entire identity around the job and tasks of early motherhood. Sure, I wanted to cherish those years, but I started thinking less about motherhood as one season and more about who I wanted to be long after the kids were out of the house. I realized whether I was with them for ten hours or one hundred hours, whether I volunteered for the field trip or had to work that day, whether they were toddlers or calling me from college, who I was could be a constant. My identity was not dictated by how well I savored the little years or how well I checked all the "good mom" boxes.

So many of the things I think add up to being a good parent aren't what I remember at all. Nate would be the first to say that his dad was far (far) from the ideal parent. He made a lot of mistakes and died at the age of sixty in poor health. Nate will laugh and tell you that, whenever he stayed with his dad as a kid, he subsisted on oyster crackers and McDoubles. Nothing was organic. There was rarely any fruit in the house. His dad was not stressing over extracurriculars or school choices. However, when Nate gave the eulogy at his father's funeral, he shared that the one thing he was absolutely sure of was that his dad liked him. Not just that he loved him, but that he liked him. His dad wanted to spend time with him. If Nate called his dad to talk about the latest Orioles baseball trade or Penn State game, he knew his dad would be thrilled to answer. Nate would say this made him feel like he could do anything and was likely the reason he had the confidence to pursue many of the dreams he had. Because his dad liked him, he didn't fear messing up; his dad's love was never dependent on how he did in the first place.

While his dad was far from perfect, Nate's identity was shaped by love. While he saw his dad make a lot of bad decisions and pay the price for them, he knew the confidence his dad had in him never wavered.

I do not have memories of my mom sitting down to play on the floor with me as a child. She had four children in eight years. She loved us, but there simply wasn't a lot of extra time for one-on-one time. I don't remember her discipline style or the way we learned chores, but I do remember how she spoke to me and the things that mattered to her. I have multiple memories where I knew she was for me and that she believed in me. Countless weekends driving me to out-of-state volleyball tournaments. Countless trips taken to look at colleges, renowned schools that I wanted to apply for and she believed I could get into.

For as long as I can remember, my mom had this gorgeous pair of gold huggie-style earrings with small diamonds in the center. They were timeless and classic. Simple enough to wear every day but also fancy enough for a cocktail party. I loved them and wanted them for my own, and I remember on multiple occasions telling my mom this and her laughing at my request. She would say, "Chyeah, right ... keep dreaming, sweetheart." And she had plenty of reasons to respond this way. It's not like they were sitting in her jewelry box never seeing the light of day; she was still wearing them often, if not daily.

The earrings became a joke of sorts.

Mom: "Kate, what's on your Christmas list?"
Me: "Your huggie earrings."
Mom: "Keep dreaming."

This sort of banter went on for years. I had one child, then two, and Naptime Kitchen was turning from a small hobby into something bigger. As it grew, I always felt weird about it. *Influencer* felt cringy. *Creator* a little less so. (At least once this book comes out, I'll be able to say *author*.) Within seconds, I can broadcast what I am up to. People have seen me dancing in my bathrobe and know what my bedroom looks like. It's like an episode of *Big Brother* got together with The Cooking Channel and made some sort of crazy hybrid show centered around a person with zero credentials.

I say all this in jest, but if I am honest, it is something I have struggled with ever since Naptime Kitchen became more than a hobby. I didn't go to school or get some degree to do what I do. I am not saving lives. There isn't a box to put this job into. It's strange work that brings a sense of both pride and insecurity. A "look at what I have built!" mixed with a healthy dose of "what in the world have I built?" I tend to have an existential crisis about it four to six times a year, usually involving tears and a needed intervention from Nate.

What am I doing? Is this the best use of my time? Am I really helping people? Am I embarrassing myself? And the biggest: *What do people think of me?* More importantly: *What do my parents think of me?*

In May of 2021, I hit a milestone in the Instagram world—100K followers. *One hundred thousand followers.* One hundred thousand individual people following a space I had created out of boredom from a tiny apartment in Durham, North Carolina. While it was a big milestone personally, it seemed like a funny thing to celebrate. But not to my mom.

Once I hit that milestone, Mom planned a dinner at a fun taco restaurant for my immediate family to celebrate. I was excited, and I also felt insecure about it. *What do my brothers think of going* to dinner because their sister has a lot of followers on the internet? Is this going to be awkward the whole time? The day of the dinner my mom was at our house for a few hours to watch the kids while I had a doctor's appointment.

That evening, when I went to get dressed for dinner, there was a small box on my bathroom vanity with a note.

I opened it slowly and burst into tears.

In it were the beloved huggie earrings.

It is hard to convey the depth of what I was feeling in that moment. Of course I was so excited to have the earrings, but what I was feeling went so far beyond the gift. The earrings marked what my mom considered to be a huge milestone in my life. In this super weird job that few people understand, with weird milestones surrounding followers, she had seen what I had been slowly building for six years. She was proud of me.

We went on to have dinner at Taco Boy, complete with a homemade crown covered in 100 Grand candy bars and a special sash. The waitress asked what we were celebrating, and my mom proudly told her, "My daughter just reached one hundred thousand followers on Instagram! You should follow her. It's called Naptime Kitchen." While I am sure I felt slightly embarrassed by the whole thing, still living in the insecurity of what my job was, something monumentally shifted for me that day. And for one reason: My mom was proud of me.

Even though the waitress had gotten off social media because it was bad for her mental health (just what you want to hear when you are out celebrating your job *on* social media), I didn't care. My mom was proud of me. And at the age of thirty-three, I needed that reminder more than ever.

While I felt awkward, she was declaring to anyone who asked that I had done something great. That evening with my siblings and parents, chips and salsa and margaritas all around, I felt bolstered to do what I do. I was believed in.

I likewise remember a time with my dad when he asked if I would consider getting business cards he could hand out to his friends with my Instagram handle on them. At the time this was hilarious to me, but it was another small drop in the bucket of my parents validating what I was doing.

These memories became a post I would tie my kite to and allow the string to go out from. Allowing myself to float a bit higher, to let the breeze take me further.

At the end of the day, my mom had absolutely no idea what the outcome would be for me and piano, or volleyball, or a million other twists and turns that happened over the next twenty-five years. Those were all things she couldn't control. What she could control (what I can control) is who she was as a person. When I look back now and think about the way my mom raised us, I am much more aware of her personhood than the specifics of how we were raised. In many ways, I wasn't seen as special. I was one of four, and we did almost everything as a pack. But in other ways, I was extremely special, because her love for me was so specific.

My mom and Nate's dad are very different. How Nate and I were raised was very different. However, we both received the same feeling from our parents. In many ways, I wonder if the boxes our parents didn't check were a catalyst for our confidence. When you have to do things on your own versus your parents doing everything for you, you stretch and grow. You fail sometimes.

As a parent, this can feel scary to me. I want to be there for my kids. I want to help them succeed. But maybe that doesn't come in the form of preparing only wild-caught salmon, volunteering in their classroom, or having a perfect discipline routine. Maybe that comes in focusing on the type of person I want to be, the character I want to have, and walking alongside my child to help them develop their own character. This can actually be harder than checking boxes. I am asking myself, *Who do I want to be long after they are gone, and what do I want my kids to see me valuing?* But it also takes a lot of the pressure off. This isn't something I have to nail or do perfectly; I am improving and evolving and messing up and apologizing and, hopefully, teaching them to do the same.

There isn't a perfect system, but while I cannot control them, I can control myself. I am still so young in this parenting journey. I think a lot of joys and heartache lie ahead. But I am realizing the best way to be a good mom is to take the laser focus off *motherhood* as my primary identity. Instead, I want to focus on who I am—who God says I am—and allow that truth to flow into all areas of life. I guess, just like my kids, I am still growing up too.

When it comes down to the nitty-gritty of how I parent, I have started to ask a few important questions to help me stay in my lane when making choices. These questions have really allowed me to lean into my own identity as a parent and be ok when others excel in an area I do not. The three questions I ask are these:

1. Are they in a different season of life than I am?

This allows me to get a better handle on how different our life stages are. The difference between having three kids under five and three kids over five is massive. Each season of parenting comes with its own set of joys and difficulties, and comparing one to another is like comparing a football player to a long-distance runner. Both train for their sport, but their training is completely different.

2. Do they have outside help?

This can be tricky, because many women (myself included) struggle to let people in on the help they have. It can quickly come across as pretentious ("Look at me with all the help I can afford!"). While there are some who want to flaunt that kind of privilege, I think the vast majority don't. I also think there is an underlying need to prove oneself in motherhood, namely because there really isn't an easy way to know if you are doing a good job. For this reason, many women (again, myself included) don't love to admit they need help. In the same way each season of motherhood is different, each person's help and need for help are different. Some women have a cleaner, others don't mind cleaning because their kids are school-aged and they have the extra time. Many women work outside the home and therefore require a nanny or daycare, while others choose to stay home. The working woman might have the money but not the time, while the mom at home might have the time but not the money. Some moms have both time and money; some moms have neither. Some are close to family, while others have none. There are so many factors going into everything from childcare to the grocery budget, and there's a 99 percent chance your circumstances are different from the mom next door.

3. Do they have the same values?

The third question is the one that I have personally found to be the most helpful: *Do we have the same values?* This question immediately allows me to take things off the "good mom" to-do list as I realize they simply do not matter to me.

These recently played out while I was making breakfast for the kids. I came across a popular homesteading blog where the mother had six children and was pregnant with her seventh (yes, seventh!). She had videos of her making from-scratch bagels for her offspring, while mine were eating frozen waffles and Cheerios. There were many differences between us, but I just kept thinking about all she was able to accomplish in a day. Taking care of six children while pregnant, making their food from scratch, even milking a cow for crying out loud.

My first thought was to question my own capacity. *Why am I unable to care for my four, while she has several more kids (and chickens, and a cow!) to care for? Why do my children eat frozen waffles while her children feast on homemade bagels?* In that moment, I stopped myself.

I literally said out loud, "Kate, she has different values than you do, and you have no insight as to whether or not she has outside help." I went about getting the kids ready for school. I realized I actually have no desire to make homemade bagels, nor to get milk fresh from a cow. While she has seven children, I am content with my four. I do not actually desire the life that she has. My face turned away from my phone to see Alberta looking up at me asking for milk. I pulled the store-bought, pasteurized carton from the fridge and poured some for her—really happy for my life.

> **MINDSET SHIFT:** Instead of focusing on who I am only in motherhood, I want to focus on who I am as a person.

MAKING IT PRACTICAL

1. Who do you want to be long after your kids are out of the house? This question has been pivotal for my journey in motherhood. When you focus on who you want to be versus the minutiae of everyday motherhood, you are focusing on something more permanent, which outlasts any one season of motherhood. I want to be a person who is patient, who is quick to admit fault and apologize, and who is present with the person in front of me. If I am a person who does these things, I will also be a mother who does these things.

2. Run any motherhood standard you come across through a filter of questions. For me that's the three questions I shared above (*Are they in a different season of life than I am? Do they have outside help? Do they have the same values?*). I follow many different

parenting accounts online, and one thing I constantly remind myself of is that each account focuses on a specific area. I follow an account that is focused on at-home kids' crafts, another about healthy food for kids, and another on Montessori learning. Each of these accounts excels in a specific area. If I am not careful, I can take on all of these different categories and pile them on to create a standard I cannot and should not ever reach. Come up with a few questions of your own to act as a filter to protect yourself from unnecessary comparison or shame. In this same vein, unfollow any accounts that make you feel shame for things that are not true moral issues. Things like nutrition, schooling, and screen time are important areas that you as the parent get to make decisions about, but be wary of any account that turns these decisions into virtues.

3. Take time to reflect on your own parents. What did your mom do that you remember? When you think about your own standards for motherhood, are they shaped by your own upbringing? Is that a good thing or a bad thing?

4. Something that has really freed me up is letting go of the notion that I want to avoid any regrets in my parenting. When I start to live under the burden of "Make sure you do the right thing here! You don't want to miss this opportunity!" I start to feel crushed. My kids are growing by the second, and there's simply too many recitals and sports games and field trip chaperone opportunities to be at them all. Sometimes I will miss an event that was no big deal, and other times I will miss something that, in hindsight, I realize was very important. But that's just it: hindsight was what made it clear. There was no way to know until after the fact. Coming to terms with regret, and living that out in front of your children, is a really healthy way to teach them how to deal with disappointment and how to own our mistakes when we make them. I am also learning

a deep balm to regret is saying "I am sorry." When I can see a mistake I made or know what I said to my child was deeply hurtful and I go apologize, there's a reconciliation that takes place, a restoration that overpowers the regret.

5. Take time to sit down with your spouse and talk through what expectations you have for yourself in motherhood. It could be that you are carrying more than you need to and placing expectations on yourself no one has asked of you (preaching to myself here—I love to feel like a martyr!). There could also be some areas where your spouse could shoulder some of the burden. I remember being so overwhelmed by all the laundry, and when I finally just expressed it to Nate, it was such an easy thing for him to start doing a few loads on the weekend. Your spouse is not a mind reader, and you are not a failure for needing help.

CHAPTER 3

I Just Wish I Had a Better Husband

> When over the years someone has seen you at your worst, and knows you with all your strengths and flaws, yet commits him- or herself to you wholly, it is a consummate experience.
>
> —Timothy Keller, *The Meaning of Marriage*

A few years ago, Nate and I got into a large argument over a smoothie cup. On that particular Sunday morning I had woken early, meal-planned, ordered the groceries, and got the kids dressed for church. I had also made a smoothie. Nate had unloaded the dishwasher, reloaded it, took Alberta for a walk, and gotten ready for church. Before leaving (which is somehow always rushed and stressful no matter how early we begin), he noted my smoothie cup in the sink and asked if, in the future, I would wash it out and not just leave it in there.

My smoothie cup was in the sink because I like to let it soak for a bit, allowing the water to soften all the dried smoothie bits before

I wash it out. Otherwise, it takes much longer to scrub. I was not being lazy, I was being reasonable. It was, of course, the practical thing to do.

What Nate saw, however, was that he had just gotten the sink clean five minutes before, and there I was leaving a dirty cup in it. He had just gotten the dishes done . . . *couldn't I see that?!* What I saw was a man noticing one small flaw and not noticing all the other things I had done that morning. I had just planned all the food we would eat for the entire week and ordered the groceries to make it happen . . . *couldn't he see that?!*

I was frustrated and snapped at him. He was frustrated by how upset I was at this small ask. I retaliated with a round of the silent treatment coupled with Miranda Priestly's "pursing of the lips" as we loaded the kids in the car to head to church. We both felt misunderstood by the other and valid in our own feelings. I remember my cheeks burning hot as we drove down Calhoun Street, indignant in my stance on the matter.

When we got to church, Nate needed to rush to serve in childcare, and I sat in the pew alone for the service. And in that space, I remembered for the thousandth time why marriage is so very hard. To live with another person and see their faults, and they see yours. To be misunderstood and misunderstand the other and continue to choose each other . . . it is hard. And yet, all over the world, people willingly choose to pick one person to spend their life with. Despite cultural changes, many of us continue to have an innate desire to find one person to commit to for life.

While Nate is undoubtedly the most amazing man—and I am so grateful I chose to marry him—I am embarrassed to tell you that I have spent a lot of time in my marriage comparing him to others. I see a couple in church where the husband has his arm around the wife, gently caressing her shoulder. Nate, on the other hand, has a solid twelve inches between us. *I just wish he were more affectionate.* I see friends whose husbands know how to cook amazing and elaborate meals. Nate makes a mean frozen pizza and has even mastered sautéing chicken sausage, but he has also asked me questions such as "What even is a rolling boil?" and "How will I know if the taco meat is done?" *I just wish he were more proficient in the kitchen.* I have seen firsthand what wishing away who my husband is can do to our marriage. The complaints pile up like small pieces of tinder, and I'm standing there holding a match.

Unfortunately, fire doesn't pick and choose what it scorches. A piece of paper in the trash and a precious family photo are one and the same to the flame. Likewise, my "just wishing" leaves tiny singe marks on my marriage as a whole. I have not been married long enough to say with any authority what makes a marriage last, but I can share a few stories that have deeply shaped how I think about Nate, stories which allow me to put down the match and tinder.

The Presumption of Innocence

Our friends Grady and Tiffany had just uprooted their family and moved to a new state in order to take over Tiffany's family's ice cream business. Grady went from having a predictable nine-to-five engineering job to being a business owner and ice cream scooper essentially overnight. All of a sudden, he had inventory to stock and employees to manage, not to mention countless freezers to keep cold. The ice cream business doesn't run on the same hours as most other businesses. People want ice cream at the exact moment you want to be putting your feet up: late at night and on the hottest of weekends. Grady and Tiffany also had three children entering a new school with their own social landscapes and friendships to make. To say there were a lot of variables and a steep learning curve would be an understatement.

I got to chat with Grady in that first year when a bunch of friends all met in Raleigh for the weekend. I asked him how it was going, and how they were surviving this massive lifestyle change. Grady told me that early on he and Tiffany made a pact to give each other the absolute highest form of the benefit of the doubt for that entire first year. If Grady was working late and missed dinner, Tiffany should assume it was because he absolutely had to. If she had to cancel a date night because one of the ice cream scoopers called in sick, Grady should believe she wouldn't have unless it was absolutely necessary. If either dropped balls on the home front or the management side of the business, the other was to assume they were both doing the best they could. Basically for that entire first year of starting this new business they knew they would both mess up a lot, and for that reason they would need to forgive often and hold short accounts.

As Grady was telling me this, I realized how often I do the exact opposite with Nate. I assume the absolute worst about him in the most innocent of situations. He's stuck in traffic and will be home late; I assume he preferred to work longer in order to miss out on the four-to-six witching hour (it is more than just an hour, unfortunately). He forgets to unload the dishwasher; I assume he opened it, saw how full it was, and thought, *Nope, I'll leave that one for Kate.*

When I am quick to assume the worst about him, our marriage suffers. Tiny weeds of bitterness begin to pop up where flowers should be. And the worst part is that these stories I tell myself are built on a base of things that are not even true to begin with. Nate knows I hate unloading the dishwasher. Nate does not mind unloading the dishwasher. Nate knows unloading the dishwasher is a massive service to me. Nate knows I am generally in a happy, more grateful mood when I go to load the dishwasher after breakfast and it is empty. Nate likes when I am in a grateful and happy mood. Unloading the dishwasher is a small lift for him with a large payout.

So why would I assume that this man would purposely look at the dishwasher and choose not to unload it? The more likely option is that he forgot. And if he forgot, I should be very quick to forgive him, because I forget things all the time.

In the judicial system (Nate is a lawyer, after all), there is something called the "presumption of innocence." What this means is that in trial, the defendant is presumed to be "innocent until proven guilty." The way to prove someone is guilty is through evidence.

Nate enjoyed his job as an attorney, but it was very demanding and draining. He left early in the morning, always tried to make it home in time for dinner, then worked most nights after the kids went to sleep. On a day he was coming home late, I could be quick to assume he was working late on purpose, that he would rather be at the office. Mind you, there was zero evidence to support this. Every waking moment of the weekend he wanted to be home and be with us; most weekdays he left work on time if not a few minutes early to try to beat the traffic. It made no sense that after being at the office all day, he would choose to stay there instead of coming home to kids he adored and a home-cooked meal. He had done absolutely nothing to lead me to believe he would choose his desk over a hug from his three-year-old.

And yet, I can be so quick to proclaim him guilty. An objective judge would see the situation clearly, but as a sleep-deprived, overstimulated wife, I would hammer down that gavel every single time. *Guilty!* I do not know why I am so quick to do this; why is my gut instinct for this person I love and have chosen to spend my life with not the presumption of innocence?

Lately, this has happened a lot when it comes to Nate's phone. If Nate doesn't answer when I call, I assume he does not care. Ironically, his phone is usually on silent or in do not disturb so that he can be more present and not constantly distracted by notifications (we really are caught by conflicting priorities when it comes to technology). I want him to be completely at the ready and undistracted when I call, but also completely dialed in and attentive when I am talking to him in person. Also, it should be noted that I miss his calls all the time.

A few years back Nate got into a horrible car accident on the Ravenel Bridge in Charleston. He was cut off and spun out before slamming into the guardrail of the bridge, bringing oncoming traffic at 5 p.m. to a standstill. Following all of this, he kept calling me, but my phone was inside. Finally, he called a neighbor who walked over to let me know what was going on. Despite my not answering his call at the time he needed me the most, he was calm and told me that he needed me to come and get him. As I drove over the bridge, I could see the fire trucks and blue lights and the massive line of cars backed up, trying to get home. And all I could think about was how I didn't answer the phone when he kept calling.

When I finally was able to pick him up, he did not chew me out. I apologized profusely, and he simply said, "It's ok. You didn't have your phone on you." Obviously, I felt terrible. I had missed my husband's call at one of the times he most needed me to answer. But him chewing me out, making me feel worse for something I already felt regret over, would not have helped the situation at all. Instead, he forgave me. He knew that I would never ignore his call on purpose. There was no evidence to support that claim, and therefore he wasn't angry with me. In that moment, he presumed my innocence, and that one act made all the difference.

The Good Stuff

There's a scene in *Good Will Hunting* where Sean Maguire (played by Robin Williams) is in his office talking with Will Hunting (played by Matt Damon). Sean is the therapist charged with the task of helping mathematical genius Will get back in line while on parole. In one therapy session, Will tells Sean he has a girl he really likes, and Sean asks about a second date. The conversation goes like this:

> Will: "But this girl is, like, you know, beautiful. She's smart. She's fun. She's different from most of the girls I've been with."
>
> Sean: "So call her up, Romeo."

Will: "Why? So I can realize she's not that smart? That she's ... boring? ... This girl is like ... perfect right now, I don't wanna ruin that."

Sean: "Maybe you're perfect right now; maybe you don't wanna ruin that. But I think that's a super philosophy, Will. That way you can go through your entire life without ever having to really know anybody."[1]

Will loves the idea of the girl he is with. He would rather keep a distance and maintain her perfect image than risk getting to know her better and learning her flaws.

Sean touches at a deeper shame we can only assume Will feels about his past. He was in and out of foster care until he turned eighteen, never having anyone love him and stick with him besides his friend, Chuckie.

There's a long pause. Will knows that Sean is being sarcastic, but he's not convinced getting to know this girl is worth the risk. Sean then breaks into a story about how his deceased wife used to fart when she was nervous. They both burst out laughing, and it's the first time in the movie you see Will truly laughing with Sean. He is enamored with this story of Sean's wife. They are both cackling to the point of having tears in their eyes as Sean remembers a particular time she farted so loud she woke both the dog and herself up. And then Sean goes on to tell Will that that's the stuff he remembers:

Wonderful stuff, you know, little things like that that happened. Those are the things I miss the most, the little idiosyncrasies that only I knew about. That's what made her my wife. [...] People call these things imperfections, but they're not. Oh, that's the good stuff. And then we get to choose who we let into our weird little worlds.[2]

We all, for better and for worse, have two sides. We have the side we present in public, and the side that lets our guard down to show who we really are. I call the latter the life "behind the curtain"—it's those parts hidden from public view. You don't have to live with someone for long before you see the behind-the-curtain part of their life, the weird-little-world side.

I do not know what my friend Lindsey's husband, Josh, does when he wakes up in the morning. I do not know if he stays up late or wakes early. I also do not know what his biggest dreams are or what keeps him up at night. I do not know any of these things, but Lindsey does. She also knows the complexities surrounding his family dynamic and what college was like for him. Lindsey is let in on all the oddities that make Josh tick. In turn, Josh is let into what makes Lindsey tick. I know the forward-facing side of Josh, the part he chooses to show around other people. But Lindsey, she knows the man backstage. When we get to know someone, to really know someone, we get let in behind the curtain. It is one of the scariest places to be, and also one of the most sacred.

When you see someone behind the curtain, for who they really are, it's as if you are seeing them without clothes on. Sure, sex is the physical side of this in marriage, but the emotional side is just as, if not more, important. All the layers we put on in public to be loved and accepted are stripped away behind the curtain. Nate gets a front row seat to my meltdowns and my insecurities. He gets the brunt of my wrath when I am on my period and sees me at my weakest moments when I lose it on the kids. But he also sees me in my deepest moments of joy and laughter. He was there to see me become a mother, and he likewise sees the excitement on my face when I come up with a new recipe. He sees me late at night, sitting in the bathtub, laughing as I rewatch *Friends* for the twentieth time. When you're behind the curtain, you get to see it all.

In his book *The Meaning of Marriage*, Tim Keller writes this:

> To be loved but not known is comforting but superficial. To be known and not loved is our greatest fear. But to be fully known and truly

loved is, well, a lot like being loved by God. It is what we need more than anything. It liberates us from pretense, humbles us out of our self-righteousness, and fortifies us for any difficulty life can throw at us.[3]

Marriage requires us to love the person behind the curtain. It asks us to attempt to love someone as Christ loves us. It is very hard to remain self-righteous in marriage for long, because that other person gets a front row seat to your weakest moments. Even as I write this book, I have personally been in one of the most demanding seasons of my life. My children are at ages where two have high physical demands and two have high emotional demands, I have work projects that require my attention, and everyone still has to eat. When I am my most stressed, I do not jump on social media to broadcast a meltdown. Nope, those are reserved for Nate to enjoy. I want to say "Lucky him" in jest, but in reality I do think it is "Lucky him." He gets to see all of me, the real me.

In marriage, we get the opportunity to see someone fully and love them. Likewise, someone sees us in all our flaws and loves us. Nate knows what motivates me and what my deepest fears are. He is the one there when I uncover a new depth of insecurity inside myself. He knows the nakedness of my heart. In a plan only God could design, he also knows my naked form. Nate sees my undressed, post-partum body when I feel like a shell of who I once was. I, likewise, see his "dad bod" as it ages. If only those two twenty-four-year-old babies on their honeymoon had any idea the perky breasts and six-pack were not there to stay.

But this is the beauty of marriage. You get to be the one let behind the curtain. You get to be the one who shows the gospel to your spouse. As Timothy Keller writes, "The gospel is this: We are more sinful and flawed in ourselves than we ever dared believe, yet at the very same time we are more loved and accepted in Jesus Christ than we ever dared hope."[4] You get to portray acceptance and love not based on performance, and in turn another preaches the same to your own heart.

When Nate and I had been married almost ten years, I went through a dark season of daily intrusive thoughts that Nate was going to leave me for another woman. This had nothing to do with how he was treating me but rather came from a deep insecurity that who I was at my core was unlovable. The demands from our four kids and my job felt overwhelming, and Nate was often getting what little I had left over. I found myself asking him to pick up the slack I couldn't and feeling disappointed in myself for not mustering enough to do it all. I knew I was not at my best, and the lie I was believing was that Nate loved me for what I could do for him, for how I served him and our family. The voice in my head whispered, *You know you aren't good enough. And soon enough he will realize it too. And then, he will leave you.*

I knew that, if I told him, his first instinct was going to be to feel defeated, to believe he had been doing something to cause me to feel this way. I asked my close friends for advice, and my friend Molly said something that will forever change how I view marriage. Molly shared that Nate, as my husband, could be an agent of healing in my life; he could combat the patterns of achievement so deeply ingrained in me simply by loving me when I am not achieving anything.

This was a breakthrough for me. I knew from our vows that Nate was to "love me like Christ loved the church." To me, this meant to love me no matter what. But what Molly helped me to see was that in loving me, Nate could redeem the lies I had listened to about who I was. In drawing me close when I felt unlovable, Nate was reminding me of God's love. He wasn't just loving me for who I was, his love could change who I was. His love, as a reflection of Christ's love, could free me from believing I had to work to be loved.

One night after the kids went to sleep, with tears in my eyes and my voice trembling, I told him what I had been envisioning. I told him I needed him to remind me often that he wasn't leaving, and to hug me more than most people would find necessary. I hated myself for telling him, for being so needy, but I needed to know that he, like Jesus, doesn't throw in the towel when life gets hard or I am no longer fun, interesting, or pretty. While Nate is not Jesus and can never fill the void of acceptance I crave, he could be an agent of redemption pointing toward Jesus as real redemption. He can love me both in spite of and because of what is behind the curtain.

Unfancy Romance

Romance with young kids is so hard. I feel like the bar gets super low, and before you know it, watching a thirty-minute show with a bowl of ice cream is a new standard for a wild Friday night. Back in college, I was part of a Christian campus ministry. During the summers we would attend a six-week program called Summer Project, where we would go live in a motel in Orlando, Florida, learn about Jesus in the mornings, and work at Disney World in the afternoons. True story: During my college years I spent two summers working at Disney-MGM Studios (now Hollywood Studios), two summers working at SeaWorld (this was in the prime years, back when trainers swam with the whales and the *Blackfish* documentary had not made its way to Netflix), and one bonus summer working at one of the country's busiest Chick-fil-As, located (not surprisingly) right outside the gates to Disney World.

All of the boys' rooms (consisting of four to five guys) were located on the first floor of the motel, while all the girls' rooms were on the second floor. We lived in tight quarters, but those summers were the most fun of my entire life. One thing everyone looked forward to was the Sunday night group date. Every Sunday night was open, and oftentimes a boys' room would ask a girls' room out on a group date for that free time slot. Everything, from the way the boys' room asked the girls' room out to the actual date, was always extremely fun and elaborate, and the cheesier the better. Gestures, like a poem recited to the girls while they sat on their balcony, were not uncommon.

Back on campus, many guys continued the theme of group dates, but no longer in a group setting. I think on the whole, this was awesome; it taught the guys a lot about planning for a date. They learned to be intentional and thoughtful. Unfortunately, this high bar made for a lot of disappointment early on in my marriage and also perpetuated the lie that all dates need to be planned and executed by the man. Not only did elaborate dates take a heck of a lot of time to plan, they also required extra cash we did not have. We were no longer in this fun college fantasy with a bunch of our friends where the only responsibility was to show up for work. We had jobs and bills to pay. Within two years, John Robert was born, and Nate started studying for the LSAT. The next thing we knew, we had two kids while he attended law school.

Dates became a breeding ground for disappointment. Eventually, Nate told me my high standards were killing him, and he was right. I also realized that I actually liked planning the dates. I had fun ideas and way more opinions on where we should go. I also had a lot more mental margin than Nate. The physical demands on me were high, but the mental stimulation from a toddler and newborn was lacking. Nate, on the other hand, sat at a desk with few physical demands but very high mental demands. I started planning more of our dates. I would book a restaurant and find a sitter. I would put it on the calendar.

The Cheesecake Factory was our place. We would eat dinner, splurge on a piece of Adam's Peanut Butter Cup Fudge Ripple Cheesecake, then walk over to Barnes & Noble to look around until it was time to head home. And you know what happened on those dates? Romance! Nate and I alone, without our children, usually with a stiff drink and lots of carbs. Even after moving to Charleston and having to say goodbye to the Cheesecake Factory, we still find ourselves gravitating to a Barnes & Noble to end a date night. While we have not been married long, one thing I have noticed is that seasons ebb and flow. Sometimes one person has more bandwidth to make the plan. Sometimes the budget or childcare constraints make dates few and far between. But the romance comes in the time together, not in keeping score of who is planning it or how elaborate it is.

The last five years have felt a bit like drowning. I remember so many times feeling like I needed a life raft from Nate, only to realize he was right next to me treading water. We are both dog tired; the kids are a lot right now. Romance feels different in this season. A swanky restaurant every so often is wonderful, but Nate picking up the toys after the kids go to sleep, or me taking the time to pack his lunch for work feels more romantic than any meal.

One thing that I think can be hard about marriage is that as a culture we are most likely going to talk about our spouse's biggest strengths and greatest weaknesses. But there's a ton of really amazing mundane acts happening in the day in and day out of life that go unnoticed. The unloading of the dishwasher, the peck on the cheek as you leave for work, the quick text letting you know he was thinking of you. So many small intricacies that make a marriage, inside jokes and memories only shared between a husband and wife.

If you type "define romance" in your Google search bar, the first definition it gives is "a feeling of excitement and mystery associated with love."[5] Dating shows like *The Bachelor* and *Love Is Blind* are highly entertaining because of the emphasis put on romance (well, and drama, if we are being honest). Everything goes great for the couple in the dating phase, away from real-life demands like doing the dishes and paying the rent. These shows center on the excitement and mystery, and it can be easy to watch and think, *Gosh, I wish my husband would take me to a private beachfront dinner in Cancun; he is such a dud.* But when these couples are faced with what real love demands, they often give up. The beachfront dinner in Cancun was fun, but she doesn't like sharing a bathroom, or he doesn't like her spending habits.

I absolutely still want fancy romance. But we have gotten a lot better at unfancy romance. Romance that is committed to the chaos of it all, together. Romance that sits with a spouse as he says goodbye to his dad for the very last time. When you can feel his heart breaking and cannot fix it but promise to be with him every day as it mends. Romance when I fall asleep on the couch, and he covers me with a blanket. Romance when I buy his favorite chips at the store, or when he makes the coffee in the morning. Romance when I apologize, and romance when he accepts my apology. Romance that you build a life on.

"For Better, For Worse"

Nate and I said the classic marriage vows you think of when you think of a wedding. "For better, for worse, for richer, for poorer, in sickness and in health." That last set always conjures up a tragic scene for me—Nate or I in a hospital bed. We have just been told we are paralyzed or have cancer. It's a miserable image, but when you are young and infatuated, you think, *Of course I would do anything for this person.* The other phrase is equally important; it says "to love and to cherish." Were one of these awful situations to play out, I am not only to stay with Nate out of duty, I am called to love and to cherish him. This could get a bit more difficult if bedpans or feeding tubes get involved. Lord willing, we never have to face a tragedy of that caliber, but you better believe we live and die each and every day by the vow "for better, for worse." I, Kate, take you, Nate, for better and for worse, in both your strengths and your weaknesses. To love and to cherish . . . for better or for *worse*.

For better or for worse, we are called to love the whole person.

One of my best friends, Lisa, is married to one of the most high energy, enthusiastic people I know. Alan, whom we all affectionately call "Babes," has been one of Nate's best friends since childhood, and we struck the jackpot when two people we loved dearly got hitched. Lisa and I laugh about how very different Nate and Babes are. Babes requires very little sleep and is always up for a fun experience. Nate loves a quiet evening and a reasonable bedtime. On New Year's Eve, when all of us were hitting a wall and ready for bed, Babes was popping champagne to fuel us until midnight. Nate and I still laugh thinking about how once the ball dropped, Babes asked Nate if he wanted to go out to the local bar down the street. Mind you, we had eight children eight and under asleep in that house, and the next morning Babes had a seven-hour drive back to DC. But Babes was having fun with one of his best friends and didn't want the night to end.

When all four of us were in the early years of marriage, I was lamenting to Lisa about some way that Nate wasn't what I wanted him to be in some scenario. Lisa very gently replied, "Kate, you can't have it all. You can't have a man who is well planned and also super spontaneous. You can't have someone who is an introvert and also an extrovert. The things you love about Nate are the very things that make him Nate. To ask him to also be all of these other things would be to ask him to no longer be the things you love about him." She went on to speak about her own husband, saying something along the lines of, "I love Alan's spontaneous spirit. It's one of the things that makes our marriage as fun as it is. In the same vein, I can't also expect him to be perfectly planned and organized. It would essentially be asking him to have a split personality."

A split personality works well for a serial killer, but it's likely not who you want to be married to. The very things I love about Nate, things like his mind, his love for reading, his even-keeled demeanor, do not go hand in hand with someone who is also impulsive and highly emotional. Being married to someone who checked all of those boxes would likely leave me exhausted and confused.

Four children later, the fact that Babes requires little sleep is one of his greatest strengths for Lisa. He can work till midnight and still have the ability to wake early with the toddlers. He can take the night shift with a newborn. He is also one of the most fun people to travel with because he will research out-of-the-box things for the entire group to do. As I write this book, Nate's love for reading has been the biggest blessing to me. Every single chapter was first edited by him. He also perfectly balances out my anxiety, his logic quelling many of my irrational fears. For better and for worse, Nate is a whole person. I cannot take only the good and leave all the bad, nor would I want to. Half of who he is would be missing.

Compounding Interest

Compounding interest is something I can still scarcely grasp. In short, when you deposit money, it earns interest. Over time, the interest also earns interest. If you put $5 into the bank at 20 percent interest, at the end of the year you will have $6 ($5 plus the $1 of interest). The next year, you aren't gaining 20 percent interest off $5 but now off $6, which will gain a higher interest. Imagine you opened an account for your child when they were born and deposited one thousand dollars, and it earned 10 percent interest yearly. If they took the money out at age sixty-five, they would have $490,370.73. Because the initial number grows yearly, the interest does as well. The biggest component for compound interest is time. Two people can invest the same amount of money at the same interest rate, and the one who invested their money earlier will have a larger sum simply because the money has had more time to compound.

At the age of thirty-five, I can hardly imagine all the intimacy that comes with getting to know another person over decades. I know my dad as Dad, but I don't know college Robbie, or just-out-of-grad-school Robbie, or brand-new dad Robbie. My mom does, though. She knows each life tucked beneath the one above it and gets the privilege to see each iteration of who my dad has become. Our lives are like a Russian nesting doll, with each past experience hidden beneath the next. Nate knows all those iterations of me. I like to think that each year or season adds a new layer, and the marriage compounds because it houses not only this new layer but all the layers beneath. The love is not based on one new thing but rather on years and years of shared experiences. When you choose to be patient, or give grace, or invest in a romantic trip, it not only produces gains for that year but gains for the marriage as a whole. The investment compounds year over year. When I think about it that way—that I get to see each new layer of who Nate is becoming and also be well versed in the layers beneath, that each year could compound on the one before it—growing old with someone feels exciting.

"You Too?"

There's a quote by C.S. Lewis on friendship that reads as follows:

> Friendship arises out of mere Companionship when two or more of the companions discover that they have in common some insight or interest or even taste which the others do not share and which, till that moment, each believed to be his own unique treasure (or burden). The typical expression of opening Friendship would be something like, "What? You too? I thought I was the only one."[6]

What has helped my marriage more than anything is my friends. I am extremely lucky to have a small inner circle of friends from college, who have known me for well over a decade. These are the type of friends you call when you've got a body in the back of your trunk and need someone to help you dig a hole. That small inner circle gets a front row seat to the ups and downs of my marriage, and I take that same seat in theirs. No topic is off limits. Everything from date night ideas to painful sex postpartum is shared there.

Just this past year, all of us were able to get together for a weekend away, and within two hours we went from laughing till our stomachs ached in a "sex highs and lows" tell-all to crying as each shared the thing in life that currently felt the hardest. The beauty in these friendships comes in sharing both the good and the bad. These friends can celebrate with me when things are going well because they also know things aren't always going well. We feel normal and understood in our messy, weird feelings because we all have them.

This past year, we all sat around as one friend confessed through tears that she was afraid she and her husband were giving so much effort to the raising of their children that they were losing the romance their marriage once had. She expressed her fears that when the kids head off to college, she and her husband will look at each other and have nothing in common anymore, that the romance will be gone. As she spoke, multiple friends expressed similar fears in their marriages. While no one had a perfect answer, there was so much peace to be found in realizing others felt similarly, that she wasn't the only one. And spoiler: Every single friend has difficulties in her marriage. Every single one has complex feelings around sex. Every single one has a complicated relationship with her aging body.

I have managed to make friends locally who fit this bill. In a newer relationship, I usually test the waters by throwing something more vulnerable out there to see how she responds. Some are quick to understand and share in turn; others nod and smile and eventually change the subject. Sometimes the latter interactions are awkward, but I never know until I try, and more often than not the other person has something to share and they are looking for a friend to confide in. As women, we so deeply want to have it all together. We fear that sharing a weakness will alienate us, when I have found it actually does the opposite. The few times I have chosen to go a layer deeper and share something more vulnerable about my marriage on Instagram, the comments come pouring in. They are all under the same umbrella of "Wow, I thought my husband and I were the only ones who fought about small stuff like this or struggled with that." All have the same refrain of "I am glad I am not the only one; it makes my marriage feel more normal." There are so many women out there desperate for this kind of intimacy in friendship, so many women believing they are isolated in marriage struggles that are anything but unique.

Having deep, meaningful friendships helps my marriage because it reminds me that I am not alone. The struggles I face are not my own unique burdens. I am reminded that others struggle like I do, and I don't have to hide the hard parts of my marriage out of shame. More often than not, when I put myself out there, I find a friend who says, "What? You too? I thought I was the only one."[7]

> **MINDSET SHIFT:** Marriage allows me to see the full personhood of my husband—the deep stuff only a spouse can know. This means I get a front row seat for the good and the bad, just as my spouse has a front row seat for me. When we daily choose each other, give the presumption of innocence, and love the whole person, over time our love not only grows but compounds.

MAKING IT PRACTICAL

1. The Presumption of Innocence: Is there an area in your marriage where you are holding back the benefit of the doubt? Is there a lie you are believing about your spouse that there isn't good evidence to support?

2. The Good Stuff: Make a list of some funny things about your spouse that you love. Maybe share that list on your next date. Take a little time to reflect on all you know about your spouse. Think about all the seasons of life you have been through together, and dream about all the seasons to come.

3. Unfancy Romance: Who in your marriage has more bandwidth right now? Are there things your spouse is doing that are trying to convey romance, even though it might not appear that way? How can you communicate this to them?

4. "For Better, For Worse": What are some qualities you love about your spouse and also some pain points? Are the things you love at odds with the pain points? Are the pain points areas that you are personally strong in?

5. "You too? I thought I was the only one":[8] Who is a friend you can trust? Make a point to confide in that person this week about your marriage and how it's going. Are you lacking friends to confide in? Don't be afraid to make the first move in friendships that go deep and allow you to know and be known in the area of marriage. Whether it's a phone call with a best friend who lives far away or a coffee date to get to know someone better, I really believe you will find that if you make the first move in vulnerability you will discover far more people who feel similarly to you than feel differently.

CHAPTER 4

I Just Wish I Had More Friends

> We sometimes choose the most locked up, dark versions of the story, but what a good friend does is turn on the lights, open the window, and remind us that there are a whole lot of ways to tell the same story.
>
> —Shauna Niequist, *Bittersweet*

There have been two points in my life when I felt like I was completely starting over with friendships. The first took place when I left for college. I burned a lot of bridges leaving high school, foolishly choosing to hang out with my boyfriend at the time instead of investing in my girlfriends. I arrived at UNC-Chapel Hill knowing no one, and that first semester, I spent every weekend I could at one of two places: I would either drive to Charlotte and stay with my aunt and uncle or drive off campus and go read at the Borders Bookstore on 15-501. By the grace of God, they let out-of-state freshmen have a car, and that was my ticket away from campus. While most students lived for the weekends, I dreaded them. Weekdays felt scheduled and safe. I had classes to attend and homework to do. But come Friday night, the realization that I had few to no plans would set in. I would go to the dorm common area and see large groups of people hanging out, so many freshmen having known each other from high school. The freshman dorms all had outward-facing hallways with sand volleyball courts at the bottom, and every so often I would get up the courage to try to join a game to make a friend. College was supposed to feel like freedom, but I was trapped by loneliness.

I was the outsider. People had their groups, and I was the one trying to break in; I was the one who needed a friend. Eventually, I rushed a sorority and joined a club or two and made friends on my hallway, but I can still remember the pit in my stomach every Saturday of that first semester. I had all the time in the world and no one to spend it with. I was accepted to the school, but I did not feel any true sense of acceptance. I was homesick, crying myself to sleep those first few months.

By sophomore year, I finally had people to spend that time with, and over the next three years those friendships took on deep roots. There was a richness and depth that can really only happen in the vacuum that is college. Living together, walking to class together, staying up all night studying together. College is a greenhouse for friendships. Like many of our friends, Nate and I stayed around the area where we went to college for six years after we graduated. Four of my college besties got married within a year of me, and we all navigated those early seasons of marriage together.

What I remember most is how absolutely broke we all were, yet how fun it was to be in that phase together. We all had rental apartments, secondhand furniture (which juxtaposed immensely with the brand-new cookware from our wedding registries), and lots of free time. Nate and I were offered a hand-me-down couch from friends who were given the couch from their parents' basement. It was at least fifteen years old, but all we had to do was drive it two miles to our duplex, and it would be ours. We were going under the speed limit, cautiously inching our way, when one of the couch sections caught wind and fell off the truck, smashing down on Hillsborough Road. For the next four years we would use that same couch with a gaping hole in the back, patched with duct tape. We would get together with our friends and eat cheap food on shiny new platters while sitting on mismatched furniture patched with duct tape, and no one cared.

After Nate graduated from law school, we left those friends back in North Carolina to be closer to family, and it quickly became apparent that while we were suddenly family rich, we were friendship poor. You might have expected me to have had lots of high school friends to reconnect with, but in truth I had none. I was starting over, navigating the mom-friend territory for the first time, and found myself alone at the park way too often. I quickly learned these sorts of friendships took much more time to grow because they involved one million more interruptions. One minute you're attempting to cross the line into vulnerability, and the next you are cut off when a child falls and scrapes their knee. There's blood, you have to pause and get a Band-Aid, and just like that, the moment for connection has passed. If college friendship was a greenhouse, making mom friends was rocky soil in a dry climate.

I decided to cast the friendship net as wide as I could and just see which ones stuck. I would casually meet someone at the park, inquiring about the age of their child. As we got to talking, if they seemed nice and lived in my general area, I might ask for their number, telling them I would text them should we come to the park again (little did they know I was at that park *every single day*). When they left, I would pull up the notes app on my phone and write down everything I remembered from our conversation. "Christina—son, Jacob, 15 months—husband, Dan, in medical school—from Ohio." I was a straight-up stalker when it came to those little notes. Had any of them ever seen it, they likely would have reported me. But you better believe the next time I met Christina she would be so impressed that I remembered her husband's name and asked when her parents would next be visiting from Ohio. Maybe Christina would become a good friend, maybe not. Either way I got one less lonely park date out of it.

Eventually, a few started to stick. One park date led to two, and eventually a meetup at the aquarium. Maybe you hit second base (lunch at Chick-fil-A) or even third (dinner at one of your houses, where your husbands met for the first time). If the men also got along, you knew you had a home run: couple friends!

After our fourth child, Alberta, was born, I was in way over my head battling awful postpartum anxiety. My friend Kristen, whose child attended the same elementary school as our son John Robert, offered to bring him home from school for me. That day, when she dropped him off, I walked out with my hair a mess, spit-up on my shirt, and still in my pajamas. It was 4 p.m. Within the hour she sent me a text saying she would bring him home every single day for the next month. Apparently my 4 p.m. pajamas and general lack of hygiene were sending an SOS signal. In a lot of ways, this one-sided favor made me uncomfortable. I could not repay her (literally, my car could not fit both her children and my own), and I felt deeply indebted to her. She assured me it was easy for her; she had an extra seat and was going to the school anyway. A few weeks later, another friend in the neighborhood offered to take Scout and Millie to preschool for me. She happened to have two extra car seats in her car from a weekend playdate and said she could easily grab them. One time turned into a week, and the next thing I knew she offered to take both of my girls to and from school every single day for the rest of the year. Like Kristen, Lindsay said she had extra seats and was going that way anyway. This felt small on their end, but for me it was monumental. I was again in a situation where I couldn't repay the favor.

Most of my life I had been in a place of being on the giving side of a friendship, or at least where the balance felt equal. *You have my child for a playdate? Ok, I will have yours next week.* I feel much more comfortable there. The receiving-only side was foreign. The balance felt off, and I was left trying to figure out how I could even the scales. In this case, I was the "weaker" friend; I was the one with the dirty hair in need of help. Before these encounters, I would have told you friendship happens when you put in the effort and work. When you instigate and make the secret note on your phone and record the details. What I didn't realize was that what I saw as a charity case (me) in need of rescuing, they saw as a friendship. Their help was creating a friendship between us.

Because Kristen and Lindsay brought my kids home from their respective schools every single day, I saw them every single day. We had touchpoint after touchpoint, small conversation after small conversation. In the dry ground of mom friends, those daily pickups and drop-offs were the water and sunshine needed. Kids can be so good at making friends, because they have no shame going to play at the same house day after day. As adults, we feel there are social rules we need to abide by; we don't want to come across as needy. But in reality, there is a need! Friendships do require some form of investment; there has to be time and mutual touchpoints to make it work. In adolescence, the initial investment is massive. You get hours and hours together that allow for you to remain close long after the proximity is gone. There is a deep well of shared experiences to draw on. In adulthood, it gets trickier. In this case, I learned that sometimes being the one still in her pajamas at 4 p.m., the one willing to accept help, can make room for friendship to grow.

When it comes to accepting help, no greater gift comes to a new mom than the meal train sign-up. If you are not from the south, the concept of a meal train might be foreign to you. In essence, it is an online sign-up where your friends near and far can sign up for a day to bring you a meal. They can personally deliver it, have it delivered, or send a gift card. The point is to space out the meals and allow the receiver to know in advance who is coming and what they are bringing. It is genius, really. Instead of bringing five lasagnas all at once, those who sign up can choose from the days you have listed and can see if you've already got two lasagnas on the way. And how can they see if you've already got two on the way? The public list that everyone with your link can see shows just how many meals you are requesting sign-ups for and which have already been claimed. And herein lies my insecurity: the public sign-up list.

When we had John Robert and Scout, we were living in Durham, North Carolina, where so many of our closest friends still lived. Those friendships spanned the better part of a decade, and the meal train sign-ups came flowing in. I think I sent my friend Maggie over thirty emails of people I knew who wanted to be able to sign up to bring us some food. My mom came up to stay with us for the first week after having John Robert, and she was blown away by the meals being dropped off. So much so I remember her telling me that was something she was most looking forward to after Scout was born: the food she would get to eat from the meal train! And I was just as pleased. *Look, Mom! I have so many friends!* Ah, the sweet, delicious security found in a casserole.

Millie was our first baby born in Charleston and my first glimpse at having a meal train not around my closest friends. But I was rational. We had only been in Charleston a year, and I wasn't super concerned that I only had a few friends at that point. Friendships take time, and we hadn't been there that long. I was well cared for by family, but my expectations were low on the friendship side of things. However, by the time we had Alberta three years later (four years after moving to Charleston), I no longer had time as my excuse. All of a sudden, my meal train became this barometer to measure how many friends I had made. And the worst part: Everyone else could see it too.

So I did what any irrational woman with erratic postpartum hormones does: I put very, very few dates on the sign-up. *Wait*, you may be thinking, *you had a newborn. Didn't you want as many meals as people were willing to bring?* One would think. But my tactic was to put very few dates, hoping that they would all be filled, and I would feel (read *appear*) to be loved. On one occasion, my friend Ruthie texted asking if she could bring a meal on one of the days I didn't have listed on my meal train. Of course I said yes. And then you know what I did? I went on to my meal train and added that date and put in her name. For no other reason in the world than for people to know, "Hey! FYI. Ruthie does love me. She is bringing me a meal. She considers me a friend." You do not need to tell me how ridiculous this is. I am embarrassed for myself as I sit here typing it. But the way I saw it, if I only put a few slots, those few slots could be filled, and I would set up a protection against people seeing empty spaces on my meal train. Empty slots, in my mind, equaled empty friendships. Friends I should have made by now but hadn't. They were a beacon for all the internet to see: Poor Kate, she really doesn't have many friends.

As silly as this scenario may sound, the insecurity was very real and was touching on something much deeper: I longed for good friends. Sure, I had a large Instagram following, but did people actually like me? Did people in my real life want to spend time with me? And while those few slots (many filled by family members) on a meal train might have looked to the world like I had friends, I knew it was a facade.

My ego was as fragile as the newborn I was holding.

Scout and Millie recently started taking a weekly gymnastics class, and at Scout's first lesson, we saw a group of six or seven girls walk in, all in matching two-piece gymnastics outfits, high ponytails, and with glitter on their cheeks. It was obvious to me that these girls likely did competitive cheerleading together (glitter on the cheeks paired with high ponytails being the dead giveaway) and had a shared history. As I watched Scout watching them, my heart ached. No one was being unkind to her, no one was really even leaving her out, but she could sense there was a bond there that she was not part of, shared experiences she didn't share. It was her first class, so she mainly focused on the mechanics of trying to do a back walkover, but that night as she was going to sleep she asked me if she, too, could get a two-piece gymnastics outfit. Deep down she knew that she might not have the shared history or get the inside joke, but she could at least try to look the part.

I wish I could tell her that friendships get easier, but I think her hardest years are still ahead. She could get lucky like my cousin Mary Ellen, who is still best friends with the girls she went to high school with. But more than likely her friendships will take a lot of twists and turns. She will make friends, lose friends, grow apart from friends, fight with friends, and find friendship in places she didn't expect. My prayer for her is that she would find one friend she feels secure to confide in and be herself around. A friend who knows who she is and isn't afraid to call her out when she's being unkind or on the verge of a bad decision. But I get it. In the moment you don't think so much about who the friends are, you just want to be included. You are willing to shape and mold who you are to feel like you belong.

I still struggle with wanting to feel included. To me, inclusion feels synonymous with belonging. FOMO, or the fear of missing out, is really FOBLO . . . fear of being left out. A fear that someone might remember me and actively choose not to include me.

Recently, Nate and I got dinner with two of our good friends, who had the incredible opportunity to take a month to travel with their two daughters. A trip just the four of them down the Intracoastal Waterway with few set plans. What a dream!

Upon their arrival back in town, Nate and I were anxious to get dinner and hear all about their adventure. We wanted to know what places they loved, where they hoped to go back to, what went well, what didn't, etc. We grabbed dinner at a new French restaurant on our side of town, and I started hammering them with questions before the bread and butter were even placed on the table. As we sipped cocktails and devoured the details of this incredible time away, something they said in the conversation pinged me, a point I had heard another friend make less than a week before.

When recounting what went well, they said, almost in unison, "It was just so nice to have no social obligations or plans. No place we needed to be at any certain time . . . to simply miss out on things."

This grabbed my attention because less than one week earlier, I caught up with my friend Ashley, who had likewise taken extended time away with her family. When I asked her what she loved most about it, she said just being with their immediate family, with no places they needed to be or social obligations. To be "off," with no expectations on them. Again with those words: *social obligations, plans, expectations*.

"It felt like that first month of Covid when no one was doing anything, and we were all strangely ok with it. No one expected us to be anywhere," Ashley recounted. "We had so much time and no set way we needed to fill it."

In both of these stories, there was a reason my friends missed out on social obligations; they were physically too far away to be asked to come. And that reason freed them from any feeling of guilt in regretting a party. They were out of town; no one would fault them for missing plans.

But I think there is a deeper freedom still: They were not only released from any guilt but they were also simultaneously released from the insecurities that come along with being left out of social invitations. Maybe they saw a group photo of friends at brunch. They could reason that no one invited them because they were out of town. There may have been Instagram stories of all the neighborhood ladies taking their kids to the pool. That's ok, they couldn't have gone anyway; they were on vacation at the beach. They weren't excluded; they simply couldn't be there. Their sense of self-worth could stay intact.

Missing out is so much less painful when it's on your own terms. Maybe we should all just start taking month-long vacations. If only.

This concept came up again a few weeks later: I got to catch up with a friend, who I'll refer to as Laura, who was visiting from out of town. She was part of a tight-knit group of people who lived extravagant lifestyles with packed social calendars, and over coffee Laura told me she was so very tired. So much so she dreamed of moving. To Laura, physically relocating her entire family to find some respite felt easier than saying no to social invitations. But we both knew she would never actually move. The fear of missing out outweighed the desire for slowness and respite. Her sense of belonging was tied to her showing up for any and all social gatherings. She was afraid that if she stopped going, she would stop being invited. If she slowed down, she might lose her friends.

And while I can look at Laura's situation and shake my head, I know that I am more like her than I realize. And herein lies the complexity of it all:

We want more margin, but we also want more plans.

We want more time for rest, but we also want to be included.

We want to say no, but we also want to be invited next time.

When the COVID-19 pandemic started, I think the majority of us, aside from first responders, really didn't know what was going on, and certainly no one was thinking it would last as long as it did. That first month was scary and stressful in so many ways, yet it was also weirdly enjoyable. We all had the same excuse to cancel any and all plans. We all had ample time to . . . well, do nothing. Work from home! In pajamas! People were out walking with their dogs and their kids in the middle of the day, waiting for their sourdough to rise.

America collectively exhaled. No one was having a fun get-together without you, because no one was having a fun get-together period. There truly were no plans. And I think that's why my friend Ashley likened her time away to that first Covid month. There was much-needed rest that came when the obligations disappeared, when the fear of missing out disappeared. Scrolling Instagram no longer brought get-togethers you weren't included in but rather from-scratch baking and Wordle scores.

But no one is trying to go back to lockdowns and restaurant closures. After two months of it we were all itching to be together again. And I think summer of 2020 brings us back to the complexity of being a human.

We loved the margin, yet we missed having plans.

We had more time for rest, yet we became restless.

We didn't have to say no, yet we missed the invitations.

I feel the tension of it too. I love a night at home with no plans and likewise feel insecure when I see a photo of friends at a place I wasn't invited to. I want free nights with no plans, but I want them on my terms.

I still struggle with this. There are tight-knit groups that I am on the outskirts of and countless birthday dinners I am not invited to. While I still communicate daily with my college besties, they are not physically nearby. In some ways, Naptime Kitchen has become a protective bubble I can hide my ego in: *I didn't get invited to that, but it's ok, lots of people on the internet appreciate me* or, more narcissistically, when my ego feels especially bruised, *I don't even need their friendship; I have strangers on the internet who love me.*

Friendship is hard, and the internet has only made it more so. I think of all the studies showing how detrimental it is to middle schoolers and teens, and all I can think is how it's equally detrimental to moms sitting at home, drowning in diapers and desperate for friendship. If that's you, I want you to know your feelings are completely valid. Being left out is extremely painful, because it can eat at the core of your identity, leaving you wondering what you need to change about yourself to be included. *Am I too loud? Too boring? If we moved to a closer neighborhood, would they invite me then?* It quickly becomes an identity issue. "If it's not you, then it must be me."

Because belonging is such a heart desire, I can often forget to think with my head. I jump to conclusions and berate myself for not being more likable or soft-spoken. But I have come to realize that friendship is an area where stepping back and thinking with my head is invaluable.

When I am in my right mind, I recognize I can only be a good friend to a certain number of people. Right now, there's a very small handful of friends who, if tragedy struck, I would drop absolutely everything for and fly to wherever they were to be with them. And I would say there's a very small handful of friends in my life I would expect to do the same. The people pleaser in me wants to be everyone's favorite, but I cannot be everyone's favorite. I am learning to remind myself it's ok to not get invited on their girls' weekend. They only make houses so big, and it's hard to get a dinner reservation for a large party. As much as I want to be included, I have to remember that other friendships can flourish when I am excluded, the same way my own flourish in a smaller setting.

It took me a really long time in life to get here, and I would say it's still something I can feel insecure about. I want everyone to invite me to everything, because that would make me feel like everyone liked me, and there's nothing I enjoy more than the love and admiration of people. But popularity and admiration are poor replacements for real belonging. The movie *Mean Girls* did a really good job of juxtaposing the two: Regina George has a ton of people who appear to be friends and is known to be the most popular, but no one actually knows her. In contrast, Cady Heron has two good friends. Two friends that welcome her and know her and aren't afraid to confront her. To the rest of the school, Regina is rich in popularity, but Cady is the real winner. Cady has true friends.

I titled this chapter "I Just Wish I Had More Friends," but as I write, I am realizing that the deeper feeling I am searching for is belonging. Whether I have one friend or twenty, what I want to feel is that there is a place for me, that people want to know me and be known by me. I want to be included, to be loved in a way that is separate from that of a partner or a spouse. I need someone to help when Nate and I are in a dry patch, arguing often and unable to see our own mistakes. I need someone who I can confide in when I am feeling really down at three months postpartum and having dangerous ideations. I need someone to hold my hand, look me in the eyes, and lovingly tell me I have been acting like a spoiled brat. A busy social calendar or full meal train are great, but they are not the best barometers for friendship.

When I feel left out or wanting for more friends, I want to do a better job of asking myself why this is. Chances are, I am not actually desiring more friends, I am wishing I belonged. Chances are that being left out likely has very little to do with me in the first place; so many things that I take personally are actually circumstance-based and have very little to do with my self-worth. But on the flip side, I know that being a better friend can start with me. If I want to feel included, I need to make the first move to include others. If I want a friend to be honest with me about something hard, I have to be honest with her. There are some friendships that won't make it, and I have to be realistic about my own capacity to be a good friend and realistic with my friends in their capacity as well.

With that lens, if you were to ask me if I want more friends, the answer would be no. Not because I don't think there are a million wonderful people who I could be friends with, but rather because I know wanting more friends is a Band-Aid for what I really need. I don't want to go wider, I want to go deeper; I need to go deeper. I need one good friend, a friend to enter the dark places in my heart, to "turn on the lights, open the window" and help me rewrite "the most locked up, dark versions of the story."[1]

> **MINDSET SHIFT:** What my soul needs is not more friendships but deeper friendships. When I find myself wanting friends to belong to, I can start by making sure my friends feel a sense of belonging with me.

MAKING IT PRACTICAL

1. When was the last time you had a deep, heartfelt conversation with a good friend? If this is something lacking in your life, what is the roadblock, and how can you make it happen this week? (Note: I am not asking you to throw a party, I am simply suggesting having one conversation with one friend.)

2. If you are feeling left out by a friend, have you talked to them about it? So often feelings are hurt due to simple miscommunications. Is there a conversation you need to have in the upcoming weeks? Personally, some of my deepest friendships are the ones that have included the harder conversations. Those conversations have led to more trust and better communication overall, and in turn, a better friendship.

3. On a heart level, it's helpful for me to remember that I am not the center of the universe, much less my group of friends. Plans will go on without my being present. The night will be fun without me. As hard as this can be to hear, it's a good thing. Little good can come from believing that I am the life of the party.

4. On a thinking-with-your-head level, so many plans I am left out of likely came down to logistics. It's harder to make reservations for a large group. Many restaurants don't have seating

for more than eight to ten. Sometimes I will not be included, and it might just come down to table size. As fun as a large gathering can be, a small dinner with a few can be such a gift. When you always include everyone, it's hard to go deep with anyone.

5. Deep friendship requires a lot of bravery, but I sincerely believe that as we go deep with others, we open the door to true acceptance and belonging. Maybe it's initiating that first stroller walk to the park or the margarita after bedtime or being the first to admit that your marriage is having a hard time. Whatever it may be, be the one to make the first move. You might be surprised at the depth of friendship that can start to take root.

CHAPTER 5

I Just Wish I Looked Better

> "How old are you, please?" returned Tangle.
> "Thousands of years old," answered the lady.
> "You don't look like it," said Tangle.
> "Don't I? I think I do. Don't you see how beautiful I am?"
> —George MacDonald, "The Golden Key"

Recently, Scout had a morning where she was completely preoccupied with what to wear to school. Mind you, her school has a dress code, but it is so loose I honestly wish they didn't have one at all or went for the full uniform. It has just enough guidelines to be annoying but at the same time not enough to allow the kids to look in any way, well, uniform. On this particular Thursday, Scout wanted to wear a white shirt to school. She did have one white shirt, but it had a collar. She wanted one without a collar. Of course this was my fault. *How dare I not have a white shirt without a collar at the ready for her!* Many (many) tears ensued. When it was time to leave for school, she was a wreck. By this point the white shirt fiasco had escalated into not being able to go to school at all. Gotta love kids and their big feelings.

I decided to keep her home for an hour and take her in late. Nate left with John Robert to get him to school and took the two younger girls with him, leaving Scout and me alone at home. After some dancing and a few hugs, she started to open up about why she didn't want to go to school. Apparently, the girls in her class had started a new game at recess called "the cool girls club," and whoever was dressed the coolest got to be the cool girls club captain. Through eyes blurred with tears, Scout told me she had never gotten to be the captain. Apparently, she was never dressed cool enough. Did I mention she was six years old and in the first grade? The first grade! At six years old, my daughter was already starting to understand that there are cool clothes and not cool clothes, and that cool girls wear cool clothes and if she wants to be the cool girl she better be wearing the cool clothes. And as I sat there, having so much empathy for my daughter and anger over the situation, I realized how similar it was to my own—how similar it has always been to my own.

For all of my life, physical image—be it the clothes I am wearing or the body beneath them—has been the main way I have compared myself and looked to get ahead.

This is something I have rarely shared online for two reasons: one, who wants to hear about body struggles from a size two? "Oh, poor you, Kate. Is it so hard fitting into your standard size clothing? Must be a real challenge being able to walk into just about any store and find clothes that fit. Cry me a river." And two: it feels deeply personal. Even someone who shares her life online daily has boundaries for what people know about her. But this is a book, and you paid good money to read it. If body image is a struggle on the mountain climb to loving my actual life, then I think it's important that you get the full, unedited (pun intended) picture.

When I was in high school, I asked a friend if I could borrow her shirt, and she told me she was afraid I would stretch it out. In that moment, I realized that she saw us as different sizes. I was the larger of the two of us, and I would hurt her clothes if I wore them.

I was "too big" for them. Over the coming months, I realized more and more that size mattered, and it was a number most people wanted to go lower, not higher. The number on the tag, along with the number on the scale, held power.

I felt so much shame about my body after my friend's comment that I made a pledge of sorts to myself. No one was ever going to be able to say anything like that to me again. Why? Because I was not going to be the "bigger girl." I started eating less and working out daily. Every day of my sophomore year, I would pack a peanut butter and jelly sandwich and a bag of carrots, and after school I would come home and allow myself a one-hundred-calorie pack of Oreos. Then I would go to the gym and work out for one to two hours. And you know what? The weight fell off. (I was also sixteen and had metabolism on my side.) And people praised me for it. I got more comments like "Kate, you look so great!" than I ever had, and I relished in them. Unfortunately, you cannot maintain the lifestyle I had created without a lot of work, and sadly this lifestyle consumed my thoughts for my junior and senior years of high school.

There's a famous quote on humility that reads, "Humility is not thinking less of yourself; it is thinking of yourself less."[1] If that quote is true, then I figured I was the least humble person on the planet. I was that awful word the Bible uses and Carly Simon sings about: *vain*.

But as I wrote this chapter, I wanted to make sure I had it right, and so I looked up the definition of vain. A Google search for "define vain" describes it as "having or showing an excessively high opinion of one's appearance, abilities, or worth."[2]

But the more I thought about that definition, I realized I was less vain and instead something a bit more sad and pathetic. It's the words *excessively high* in that definition that made me realize what I struggle with is less about vanity and more about comparison and self-worth. *Do I measure up? Am I as pretty or thin or smart as (insert other females in the room)?* Ugh. As I write those words it actually sounds even more pitiful than enjoying the excessively high opinion of myself vanity would bring. I wasn't vain, I was insecure.

Looking back at photos, I was so very thin. And all I can remember is loathing my body. Picking it apart, hating myself for not having a six-pack, and being obsessed with the size of my jeans. Body size became the ultimate barometer for worth. My skin could be breaking out and my hair in a moppy, greasy bun, but if I felt thin, I felt powerful. I cringe as I write this because I do not want people to know I care so much about what I look like. I want my beauty to appear effortless. *Who, me? Beautiful? Wow! Thank you, I hadn't even noticed!*

The body issues I was experiencing in high school followed me right into college like a bad habit. Thankfully, two things happened in that next decade: I took a class where we were assigned to read a book called *The Body Project*, and I lived in a tiny apartment in Washington, DC.

The Body Project by Joan Jacobs Brumberg chronicles female body image standards from the invention of the mirror to the printing press and so on. It explains that, for the longest time, women rarely had access to see what they looked like. Eventually, homes started to get mirrors, which allowed a woman to see her own face. These mirrors, however, were still fairly small in size, and rarely did someone have one that showed her entire body. Women were likely still comparing themselves to one another, but only to those in close proximity. Then came the printed advertisement. As they grew in popularity, newspapers began to run ads for things like a women's dress shop. This ad would have a photo or sketch of a woman wearing the dresses for sale. Slowly, the shift started: What was printed in the paper was what a woman should look like. What happened next is pretty obvious: Ads in the papers grew to ads in magazines that grew to ads on billboards and now to ads on screens. But going back, I remember how much I thought about that very first step: the mirror. There was a time when the most a woman could know about what she looked like came from catching her reflection in a window. Surely she didn't notice her wrinkles; she likely barely knew what color her eyes were.

Fast forward eight years to 2016. Nate and I had been married four years, he was doing a summer internship for law school, and I was pregnant with our second child. This particular internship took us to Washington, DC, for six weeks, where we decided to splurge on the rent and live downtown next to George Washington University's campus. While Nate was at work, I pushed a then-fifteen-month-old John Robert all around that city. We saw the Smithsonian museums, the White House, and the Kennedy Center. We grabbed treats at Georgetown Cupcake and walked along the Potomac. It was like living in a dream. One cool thing about downtown DC is that stores are just sort of interspersed right around office buildings. We might be walking down a street and come across a boutique or department store squeezed right between two law firms. We were essentially broke at this time (hello, law school and splurging on a cool apartment), but I did find myself popping into Nordstrom Rack from time to time to check the clearance section. On one occasion I found a pair of shoes that I knew I would need to try on with long pants to get a better picture of how they looked. I bought them and headed back to our tiny apartment to try them on. When I got back, I threw on some jeans and searched every single closet, nook, and cranny for a full-length mirror. It was then I realized that our apartment had one mirror: a medicine cabinet bolted high above the sink in the one bathroom. I could barely get a glimpse of my growing stomach, let alone my shoes.

In that one outfit instance, I found the lack of mirrors to be a bit frustrating, but as the summer went on, I realized how completely wonderful not having a bunch of mirrors around was for me. I was newly pregnant, in that weird stage when no one really knows and you just look bloated, but I had little to no opportunities to criticize my body. I would look at myself in the morning when brushing my teeth, and then I would go about my day, rarely seeing more than my reflection in a giant office building window.

That particular summer, Nate actually split his internship between two firms: One in Charleston, and the other in DC. For the first six weeks we lived with my parents in Charleston. Their house has a giant fifteen-foot-mirror right at the entrance that is absolutely beautiful and really makes a statement when you come in the door. I remember, however, how often in high school I would use that same mirror to criticize and critique my body before leaving the house. My bedroom at my parents' house also contained a full length mirror, along with a mirror in the bathroom. It was very telling for me to have these two locations juxtaposed within a few weeks of each other. One contained countless mirrors, and the other contained just one.

Over those next six weeks in DC, I would fall in love with having very few mirrors around. Sure, there were a handful of times I really wanted to see if my shoes went with my outfit, but for the most part I absolutely loved it. I realized what a distraction mirrors were for me and how much happier I was to have fewer of them around.

When we got back to Durham, I intentionally got one of those cheap mirrors that hangs on the back of a door so I could close it off and only use it when I needed it. A few years later when we moved to Charleston, I decided to order a large, full-length mirror. I wanted that lovely large mirror aesthetic I saw everywhere online. It arrived, and I leaned it against the blank wall I would pass every single time I headed into our office. It might sound silly, but after about two weeks, I knew I hated it. Nate even made a comment, saying he didn't love seeing a giant reflection of himself every time he entered the office. So, I returned the giant mirror and got a smaller one from Home Goods that now sits in the corner of our bedroom. In order to see myself in it, I have to physically go to the other side of the room and stand in front of it. That large wall that leads into the office now has a giant print hanging on it, which Nate and I both agree is so much more enjoyable to look at than our own reflections.

Reflections have an incredible effect on a person. In the world of editing apps and Instagram filters, they are one of few things that give us an accurate view of what we look like. On the one hand, this is a very good thing. We need to see ourselves outside of a screen. But on the whole, in every season of my life when access to a mirror has been limited, my life has been the better for it.

Nate didn't like the mirror in the office for a very different reason than me, and it's funny how God often has us marry someone who so perfectly complements our own struggles. Nate is one of the least physically self-aware people I have ever met. Mentally, he is sharp as a tack. He cares to know what is going on in the world; he reads daily and sees the value in knowledge. But when it comes to physical appearance, the man couldn't care less. I don't mean to say he doesn't shower or brush his teeth, but he is truly not concerned with current trends or if he has a six-pack at the beach. His disdain for being on trend is almost to the point of bucking anything deemed new and cool, and sometimes I want to slap him for it. However, his own lack of care has always challenged me because of how much I do care. I didn't want the giant mirror because I am overly concerned, and he didn't want it because he thought the space could be used for something much more useful than his own reflection.

While what Nate saw in the reflection wasn't a struggle for him, he did have a life event that pushed him to get into better shape. When Nate was thirty-two, his dad passed away suddenly. He had complications from a surgery that his organs could not recover from. Unfortunately, his dad had never taken care of himself, and had he been in better shape, he likely would have made a recovery or at least been eligible for a second surgery. He was sixty years old.

This massive loss served as a wake-up call of sorts for Nate, not for the sake of looking good, but because he wanted to live to meet his grandchildren. Nate decided on a goal: He wanted to lose ten pounds over the next ten years. When he told me this goal I made fun of him for months. Ten years? What is the point in that?

In Nate's mind, if he could lose ten pounds over a decade as opposed to gaining somewhere between ten and thirty, he would be all the better for it. Because the goal felt so small, he started small. He began to run one mile every morning. Never more, just one mile. After about a year of this, he decided to add in ten minutes of yoga (mostly to help improve his mobility for his golf game). Somewhere in there he decided to stop snacking late at night and made a goal to not eat past 7 p.m. Around six months later, he opted to nix the weeknight bourbon and only have one on the weekends. Mind you, these small changes happened over a three-year period. And over that time, he lost over twenty pounds. In three years, he had met his goal and then some, but not in the way people tend to think.

His goal being so small and incremental was why it was so successful. He didn't attempt to start running, doing yoga, fasting after seven, and nixing the weekly drinking all at once. Each decision came in its own time, usually after another decision had become a fully formed habit.

I found this especially challenging because it went so deeply against the way I choose to do things. I am much more grand, more all-or-nothing. Why train for a 5k when you can try for a marathon? That's my motto. The problem is a marathon is much, much more intimidating. It's easier to talk yourself out of a ten-mile run than a one-mile run. Small habits are easier to say yes to, and therefore easier to maintain. It's now been five years since Nate started his morning run habit, and Monday through Friday you can find him on his one-mile loop. Maybe he will run longer one day, but he says he's really content with the mile. The way he sees it, if he's still running a mile a day and doing yoga at forty, he'll be better off than most of the men his age.

I have started to think about my own health journey more like that: as something I want to continue over the long haul versus a quick fix for a certain body type. Maybe it's aging, maybe it's a better perspective, but I have found myself thinking more about what will allow me to feel good over the next five years rather than focusing on what will make me look a certain way in the short term. I joined a high-intensity gym when Alberta was around eighteen months old, and while the workouts were killer, I knew in the long run they weren't the best for me. I often felt on the verge of injury, my knees ached, and I left feeling completely depleted as opposed to energized. I feared that what, in the short term, burned a ton of calories was going to hinder my ability to run or play with my grandchildren one day. The short-term benefits weren't worth the long-term cost. Like Chandler Bing from *Friends*, I marched right in there and proclaimed, "I wanna quit the gym!"[3] I still exercise every morning, but in a way that feels much more sustainable. Do I have a six-pack? I most certainly do not. But I feel healthy and strong, and if John Robert wants to play a game of pickleball I can do so without limping.

Nowhere in my life have I felt more hypocritical than in how I act when it comes to aging. I have wrinkles around my eyes and sunspots from being a young girl who spent too much time at the beach armed with nothing more than a bottle of baby oil. The skin around my knees is starting to pool like an elephant's ankle, and don't even get me started on adult acne. My phone has become a place I struggle with more now, because daily it acts as a mirror for me. I get on Instagram stories and immediately see my own face in the selfie camera. I am aging. I don't think it's helpful to see my face as often as I do, and I understand why so many slap a filter on to soften the reflection staring back at them.

Somewhere in the last few years my arms and legs started to get these minuscule bumps on them. I went to the dermatologist and she suggested a lotion to help, and it works, but it's yet another step added to the ten-step regimen. This last year I also had a laser treatment done on my face to help with acne scarring. The treatment was as expensive as it was painful and left my skin flaking off like some sort of reptile for the days that followed. For a week, I looked like a lizard woman caught in mid-transformation. While I do believe the treatment helped, within twenty-four hours of the skin peeling off and the fresh baby skin appearing, I had two new pimples. New marks on the skin I had just paid a small fortune to have renewed. In so many ways, this desire to look young and untouched by the effects of the world, things like wrinkles from smiling and sunspots from warm days spent outside, feels like trying to fill a bucket with a hole in it. I plug one hole, and a new one sprouts. It's my very own game of whack-a-mole, each new spot or ailment something I try and smash down, just for two more to pop up.

Part of me wants so badly to make peace with my body and age gracefully, to welcome the wrinkles with open arms and be ok with how I look even if people around me are not doing the same. I want to be able to detach my self-worth from what I see when I look back in the mirror. Recently I was listening to an interview between Julia Louis-Dreyfus and Jane Fonda. The podcast is called *Wiser Than Me*, and in it, Julia interviews successful, powerhouse women who have gone before her. Women she, quite literally, considers to be wiser than herself. Listening to the episodes has been very eye-opening for me, to hear what Jane Fonda has to say at eighty-five, or what Sally Field has to say at seventy-seven. In the episode with Jane Fonda, Jane admits she regrets getting plastic surgery. "I wish that I had been able to grow old at peace with my face, but I wasn't able to, and I don't feel good about it. It's not real, but I can't do anything about it now."[4] It's easy for me to see Jane and judge her, to think she only looks the way she does from surgery. But as I get older, I empathize more with where she is coming from.

I swore off Botox for years, and now I find myself at quarterly injection appointments. I like the way it takes away the wrinkles; I love how tight my forehead feels. But it's also something I struggle with. For years, I hated Botox. I hated how it made the playing field so uneven. Some are aging, while others' faces are, quite literally, frozen in time. I thought, *Aging would be so much easier if we all agreed to do it together*, like making a pact with your friends not to give the kids cell phones until they turn sixteen. But we all know how that goes. One mom cracks and her kid has a phone, and now all the moms feel the pressure to give their kids one as well. Here I am, getting my face frozen. In some of my social circles, I am the last to try it, and in others I am the proverbial mom handing her kid a cell phone at age ten. Every day I love how it looks, and every day I wonder if I am putting my hard-earned money into furthering the lie that women need to age in such a way that it barely looks like we are aging.

I have heard the advice a million times, "When you are older you will regret caring so much about what you looked like," but that is so hard to believe when you are twenty-six and everyone is caring about what they look like. In Julia Louis-Dreyfus's interview with Sally Field, Julia asks her what advice she would give to her twenty-one-year-old self, and Sally shares this same sentiment: "I would say, you know, don't worry about your thighs that much . . . I was always so worried about weight." Dreyfus goes on to ask, "Is there anything you want me to know about aging?" Sally says that "there is a sense in society that you should feel ashamed for being old" and that it is specific to women. She continues, "No matter what I do, my waist is just going to thicken. I can't make it not. I could starve myself to death and then I think, I don't want to starve myself to death anymore. It's just what age is doing and my body needs to react like this and I will still keep it healthy and I will still do what I can, but I have to constantly keep myself from [. . .] shame creeping in."[5]

It's funny how critical I can be of my own face and yet so gentle toward my mom's face. She is sixty-five, let her hair go white in her late forties, and has never done any antiaging facial treatments. To me, she is absolutely beautiful, and she looks the age she is. She has freckles and wrinkles and laugh lines. Her face and her body tell the story of all the years she has been on this earth. When I think about eighty-year-old Kate, I want her face to likewise tell a story of a life well lived, not a life spent fussing over her skin or her pant size.

While this struggle remains, the more I age and the more I listen to women much older and wiser than myself, the more I am coming to understand this is simply a battle I will not win. I can see how slippery the slope becomes when wanting to reverse the time clock. Botox turns to filler. The creams and serums only get more complex and expensive. It's an uphill battle that is ultimately lost. Maybe I will have stopped by the time this book comes out, maybe I won't. It's a strange butting of desires.

When I think about what Sally Field said, I also want to fight against any shame that would come with aging. Shame comes when you feel like you have done something wrong or foolish. When I think about growing old, it makes no sense that I would feel anything wrong about that. There is nothing criminal about growing old. If you were to meet a friend for coffee and notice the crow's-feet around her eyes or sunspots, would you think any less of her or demand some explanation for why she looks the way she does? Of course not! You would see her body as a physical vessel showing all the marks of the life she has lived. You would never ask, "Why do you have wrinkles?" You know why she has wrinkles! The same reason you do: because you are getting older and your body tells the story of all the years you have lived. As I write this, I have a tan from being in the sun all summer with my family. That sun exposure will likely result in more aging to my skin, but I wouldn't trade those warm days in the sunshine for anything. Your body is a living thing that reflects the experiences that make up your life; the day it stops aging is the day you stop living.

As I sat there with Scout, weeping over her desire to be captain of the cool girls club, I realized we were twenty-eight years apart but fighting the same battle. Clothing, wrinkles, the number on the scale . . . it all boils down to a common lie, a never-ending desire for a perfect body that does not exist this side of heaven, and a shame we should not feel.

This is an area I am still processing. I don't have the answers to aging well, but I do think the first step comes in welcoming it. Maybe it's the wisdom that comes with getting older and learning from those much older than myself, maybe it's having fewer mirrors around, or maybe it's committing to sustainable goals. One way or another, more and more I am coming to peace with my body. The high school version of Kate is still in there, but she's much quieter now. I think she's tired, and desperate to show her own daughters a different, better way.

> **MINDSET SHIFT:** My body tells the story of the life I have lived, and that is nothing to be ashamed of. I can come to peace with my body, even as I age.

MAKING IT PRACTICAL

1. For a period of time, experiment with removing unnecessary mirrors from where you live. Why does this help? You simply aren't looking at yourself or being given the opportunity to body check nearly as often. Have a full-length mirror somewhere where you can give your outfit a look-over before leaving the house but not in a primary location that you pass often.

For me, that's the corner of our bedroom. I have to walk to the other side of the bed to get to it and never pass it by accident. Have a smaller space? Consider getting a full-length mirror that hangs on the inside of a closet door. That way, you can close it off when you want to.

2. When considering any goals around health and body image, ask yourself, "Is this sustainable?" That was the key to Nate's goal. It didn't overwhelm him because it was small and sustainable. If you want to start exercising, ask what would be a sustainable goal, and begin there. Maybe it's simply ten minutes a day. Over time and in different seasons, what is sustainable could change, but you need your habitual goals to feel attainable, or you will likely get discouraged or burn out. You want your health to be for the long haul, so make sure your expectations and practices are ones that can last.

3. Unfollow social media accounts that cause you to struggle with body image. This one was big for me! I was following a few exercise-type accounts, which would constantly cause me to compare or feel like I wasn't doing enough. Because of the way social media works, I never really knew when this content would pop up, and if I wasn't in the right headspace, it would really affect me. Unfollow or mute these accounts, and only visit their page on your own terms, if at all.

4. Have one trusted friend who you tell when you are having a hard time. Not because they know the right words to say, but because sometimes when we simply say something out loud, we take the power out of it. This person could be your spouse, but I would suggest a friend, if possible. Not that you shouldn't talk to your spouse about it, but I think they could feel pressure to tell you what they think you want to hear, as opposed to a friend, who may give you more solid truth to stand on.

5. Take a moment to think about yourself as a grandmother. What do you think will matter the most to you then? Likewise, think about your own grandmother. What do you remember about her as she aged?

CHAPTER 6

I Just Wish I Had More Money

> Most people are wired to seek status and success, not necessarily happiness. It's remarkable to watch someone fight back against that trend. From the outside they appear frugal. But in fact they've rejected what the world tells them they should want and looked deeper, finding their happiness elsewhere.
>
> —Morgan Housel, "Frugal vs. Independent"

As I write this, Nate's car is struggling. It's a 2014 Subaru with windows that don't roll down and zero of the latest safety features. It runs fine, but I am fairly certain this Charleston summer is about to kill the AC. I have spent a lot of time online looking at cars to replace it (it's Nate's car, but really, it's a car we drive interchangeably whenever someone goes somewhere without the kids), and I keep coming back to the same questions.

There's a used luxury-brand car selling for the same price as a brand-new non-luxury car. The used car has more miles on it and is less up-to-date, but it's also a luxury car. It's pretty, and it has that symbol on the front to let everyone know it's luxury.

Both cars cost the same, but I am attracted to the luxury car, and I continue to ask myself why.

There are few things I have spent more time in my life thinking about than money. But likely not in the way you would imagine. It's not an obsession with how to get it but rather a constant question of what role I want it to play in my life. It is not even so much what I want to spend it on, but rather what I want it to say about me—what I want the things I buy to say about me. Who I am in relation to money. What I would be willing to spend money on and what I would deem frivolous.

The car is one example, but it represents a larger trajectory I come back to about where my life is and where it is headed, about where my values lie. Do I value the luxury logo even though it has more miles and fewer features? Do I want it because I genuinely think it's better or because it's deemed luxury? Do I care if people see that I drive a luxury car? What am I hoping to convey about myself through someone seeing me drive it? Is that what I want to convey?

Living in my head is exhausting.

My complicated feelings toward money started early. I grew up in an affluent family in Charleston, South Carolina. Charleston itself is already considered to be a very wealthy place, so to be wealthy in Charleston really puts you a tier above. I had everything I could want and was very aware of money and status. Before we go on, I realize this might rub some of you the wrong way, especially those for whom finances are a real week-to-week struggle. And for that reason, I almost didn't say some of the things I'm going to say in this chapter. But when I started writing this book, I vowed to myself that I would be as honest as I could be. So I'm going to tell some stories that might feel uncomfortable, but I think there are some lessons here for all of us—no matter which financial tier we fall in. I hope you'll stick with me.

In middle and high school, the girls I hung out with wore nice jeans and drove nice cars and had nice purses. There was a fixation on having whatever the newest, nicest items were. In junior high, it was all about jeans. I have a strong memory of my dad being so excited to take me shopping for my birthday. Sixteen was a big age, and he told me I had $200 to spend with him. He thought we had a fun afternoon ahead of us. I, however, already knew I wanted to go to The Copper Penny on King Street, and there I spent the entire $200 on one pair of jeans. My dad shook his head, our day of shopping being over in a half hour. But at sixteen years old, I knew what nice jeans were and that I wanted them. To my sixteen-year-old self, these jeans were luxury. These jeans were status.

Fashion is an area where you can't often see a big difference between premium and luxury brands. Premium brands are known to offer higher quality and better performing products. Many people might buy a premium brand product not for any sort of status symbol but because they genuinely think the item is better quality or has more features to offer. Premium would be buying a new bag because it genuinely has more pockets and better features, versus buying one simply because it has a special monogram stamped all over it. Luxury brands do offer a good product, but it is usually not of a quality that justifies the higher price point. The price point is associated with the exclusivity and status one feels in owning the product. I can say with full confidence that my jeans did not offer me $120 more utility than an $80 pair of jeans, but they had this squiggly line on the back and a small red tag on the right butt pocket that let people know they were Sevens. At sixteen, I don't think I so much understood that nice jeans conveyed wealth, but I knew they conveyed status and popularity, both of which I cared deeply about.

This fixation with nice things continued throughout high school. I didn't see it as an issue, but rather, it was the air I breathed. When friends wanted to go shopping, we went to King Street. Arguably one of the wealthiest shopping locations in the entire southeast, King Street had everything from Gucci and Louis Vuitton to more mainstream brands like American Eagle and Abercrombie & Fitch. My junior year, I got a job working at the J. Crew on King Street and would spend my paycheck almost entirely on clothing using my precious employee discount.

Since money was so closely tied to how I measured myself against others, it should come as no surprise that money was one of the biggest ways God drew me to himself. When I was a senior in high school, I was driving a new car in my nice jeans, without a financial care in the world, and I was miserable. The dopamine rush from a new outfit no longer hit the same. I was bored and restless. I started to turn toward other unhealthy pursuits like being as thin as possible and going to parties. Everything was fun for a while (except the trying-to-be-super-thin part, that was miserable), but within a few months I would feel empty again. Looking back, I completely understand why drugs are such an issue for kids with money; drugs fill a place where they feel bored and restless, a place no physical item has satisfied. These individuals don't dream of saving their money to get nice things; they already *have* nice things, and it still isn't enough.

It is important to me that you know where I came from, because it's likely the biggest factor in how I view money now. I had what so many people wanted. I had money and the security it offers, yet I felt completely insecure. I didn't have a clue what I needed, I just knew there was a void that money and what it bought couldn't fill. The desire for joy and purpose beyond money and what it could buy was so obvious it felt visceral to me. I became a bit jaded by the entire idea that being rich brought happiness. Don't get me wrong, there were a ton of amazing things I got to do and places I got to see because we had the money to do so. Money undoubtedly opened doors for me that otherwise would have been closed; I just knew at the end of the day that money and what it offered was not the answer.

College was where I had my concept of money blown wide open. I went to UNC-Chapel Hill, which coming from out of state felt both expensive and impressive but for many in-state residents was an affordable state school. On a Friday night, my roommate asked if I had a pair of jeans she could borrow (*why is so much of this chapter about jeans?!*); I told her I had some Sevens in the closet. (Reminder: In high school my expensive 7 For All Mankind jeans represented both status and style.) My roommate responded by asking if I cared which of the "seven pairs" she borrowed. She had never even heard of the brand, let alone owned a pair. It turned out status symbols only work if people recognized them. Over the next three years, I would realize that the financial bubble I had grown up in was not the norm, and that there were a million micro levels between the words *poor* and *rich*. I would come to understand that money was incredibly complicated, and people's relationships with it even more so.

Also while in college, my grandmother sent me a check for $100 with a note that said, "In case you need a little Christmas, right this very minute." I was so excited! When you are a broke college student, $100 feels like a golden ticket, and her phrasing in the note made me know it was meant to treat myself to something. I knew I wanted a new bag for travel (*wow, this whole chapter is jeans and bags*), so I went to a few stores to try them out. I labored over which to get, researching and price checking. I eventually landed on a Mountain Smith hiking bag that I still have to this day. I used it in college (things like Chacos and cool hiking bags were very *in* at UNC-Chapel Hill), and then later, after Nate and I were married, I used it for our trip to hike the Grand Canyon. I loved that bag. I appreciated it because I knew it was nice (at least nice by my broke-college-student standards) and because it was what I had used my precious "right this very minute" money on.

I can tell you right now what Nate would have done had he received that same check: He would have saved it. And therein lies one of the hardest marriage battles we have: the spender versus the saver. If ten years of marriage has taught me anything, it's that there are virtues and flaws to both ways of thinking, and ironically, that the spender and saver act like each other when they are in a healthy headspace.

Allow me to explain: In stress, the spender feels like they can never get all the things they want. There simply isn't enough money for all the things they desire. In stress, the saver feels as though they can never save enough; there is never enough to provide the security they are looking for. Ironically, the spender in health acts more like the saver. They realize they don't actually need everything and are fine to go without, and in doing so they save money. Likewise, the saver in health acts like a spender. They know they will never be able to save it all and can feel the freedom to let go and loosen the grip on their finances a bit.

After Nate and I got married we worked for a Christian college ministry for a few years, followed by Nate starting law school. Even then we were set on starting to save money, but the earnings were minimal. Basically, Nate would work a summer law internship that would pay him well, and we would live off that money for the rest of the year. I shopped at Trader Joe's, with the goal of our weekly groceries costing around $80 to $100. Our birthday lists were extensive and often included things like a new frying pan, gift cards to Starbucks, or new towels.

I knew that my grandfather was concerned about our finances. He would slip money in the mail to me, and on a number of occasions called just to make sure I had what I needed. More than one time he sent a card in the mail with a $50 bill and the words "It is time for you to come home" written on a piece of his stationery. The $50 wasn't a bribe; it was gas money to get me home. On one funny occasion, I had a ton of extra breast milk in the freezer and the prospect of selling it came up. All we could think about was how hilarious it would be if my grandfather found out. We would laugh out loud with my mom at the thought of my grandfather calling her in a fit, saying, "Berta, she's selling her milk!"

While I never ended up selling my breast milk, I learned a lot about using coupons and the power of stretching a dollar. We started asking the question, "Can we go one more day?" and would ask it often to see just how many days we could go between grocery runs. We drank Trader Joe's Two Buck Chuck and used our student IDs at the movies long after the date read they had expired.

Here's the thing: Our needs were high, but I think we were just as content, if not more so, in that season. We were extremely rich in the area of friendship. There was something beneficial about not having everything we wanted; there was joy to be found in wanting something and not getting it right away. As our bank account grew, the excitement over a $100 check in the mail lessened. That $100 didn't hold the same value it once had. Herein lies the law of diminishing marginal utility. The more money I had, the less joy each dollar was able to bring me. It's not that more money was bad, it just didn't equate to more joy like one might expect.

Money is extra tricky, because it's not the money itself that traps us. We have seen when a nation's currency gets devalued and becomes worthless. Physical money is flimsy paper and coins, but it's what we can get with it and what it represents that makes it valuable. This makes it very different from other loves. You love someone and get married, not for what it can get you, but because they are the person you want to be with. You have children, not for what they can get you or say about you, but because they bring you joy. Money is different; money is simply a currency to get what we really want.

It's good for me to look back and remember seasons of surprising contentment that arose even when money was tight. Those seasons remind me that we don't need to constantly move the goalpost when we hit a financial goal. Have you heard of that phrase? In football, the goalposts are fixed at the back of the end zone, and the goal of football is to reach the end zone and score a touchdown—but imagine if they kept moving. If they kept being pushed further back, you would keep working down the field but would never score a touchdown.

When it comes to money, it's the equivalent of never feeling like you have enough. Maybe what you want is to afford a decent house and a car for your family to drive, but then once you get those things, the goalpost moves. Now you want a larger house, or a house in a nicer neighborhood. You no longer want the average car, you want a luxury car. Wealth is built by not allowing your lifestyle and spending to expand as your earnings expand.

Not moving the goalpost seems easy, but it's sneaky and difficult. You slowly start to be able to buy better clothes and more expensive groceries, and you eat out more. Maybe you really can afford a better car or take on a heftier mortgage. You can, so you do. And it doesn't happen all at once. You don't go from spending $2,000 a month to $10,000 overnight. It's slow. Like the proverbial frog boiling, the water around you continues to heat up one small degree at a time, until the next thing you know you're spending ten times what you used to.

Unfortunately, you are not ten times happier, because contentment does not work like we think it will. It's like a mirage on the horizon, ever so slightly out of reach. And if what we want is ever so slightly out of reach, oftentimes the money to make it happen is ever so slightly out of reach as well. If my spouse just made a little more money, if bonuses were just a little larger this year, then we would really be happy.

In his book *Fooled by Randomness*, Nassim Nicholas Taleb tells a story of a well-to-do lawyer (Marc) living in New York City with his second wife (Janet) and three children. He works all the time, makes half a million dollars a year, and is able to afford all of the wants and needs for his family. Unfortunately, the apartment building they live in on Park Avenue is also the home to Wall Street traders and corporate executives who make ten times his annual salary. Despite making more money than 99.5 percent of Americans, in this apartment building, Marc and Janet are at the bottom. Taleb describes the social treadmill: "You get rich, move to rich neighborhoods, then become poor again." He goes on to explain that while he wishes Janet's knowledge that she and her husband are among the top 1 percent of Americans would satisfy her feelings of inadequacy, "becoming more rational, or not feeling emotions of social slights, is not part of the human race." Taleb believes what would actually make Janet happier, at least when it comes to comparison, would be to move to a neighborhood where they are some of the most wealthy.[1]

Going off Taleb's story, I agree that, on the whole, people with nicer houses in average neighborhoods are happier overall than people with average houses in nicer neighborhoods. Why? Because the person with a nicer house surrounded by less nice houses has a perspective that says they have more than enough, whereas the person living in the less nice house in a neighborhood of super nice houses has a perspective that they are lacking. Your perspective is formed by what you are living around.

One unfortunate side effect of the internet is its power to broaden your "neighborhood." With access to photos and videos across the world at your fingertips, you can surround yourself with "neighbors" who have much more disposable income than you (or at least look like they do), and all of a sudden it can feel like you are lacking. You've got a bunch of rich friends you don't even know and a goalpost that needs moving to keep up.

In writing this book I did a little research on "Keeping up with the Joneses" and learned that the phrase actually originated from a popular comic strip titled, you guessed it, *Keeping up with the Joneses*.

One particular strip summed up so well what I believe many of us so often feel: [2]

It's that small little phrase that I so quickly believe: "She gets something out of life."

I believe that because another person has a larger house, a nicer kitchen, or a better car that they are getting more out of life.

I know money can't buy happiness, but I still find myself just like Clarice. Money might not buy happiness, but it might just buy me a little more than I currently have.

As luck would have it, if I am Clarice, then that makes Nate Aloysius P. McGinis. But in our version of the comic Nate would respond with something along the lines of "Tough luck, Clarice."

In his book *The Psychology of Money*, Morgan Housel writes, "People with enduring personal finance success—not necessarily those with high incomes—tend to have a propensity to not [care] what others think about them."[3] Sounds easy, but I think this is very, very hard, especially for women. My daughter Scout is seven, and I already see her looking around, wondering how she measures up to those around her. Add in the millions of dollars put into advertising to make her believe she needs more clothing, better skin care, and nicer things, and it's no wonder money is such a struggle.

Again, Housel writes this:

> The hardest financial skill is getting the goalpost to stop moving. ... Modern capitalism is a pro at two things: generating wealth and generating envy. Perhaps they go hand in hand; wanting to surpass your peers can be the fuel of hard work. But life isn't any fun without a sense of *enough*. Happiness, as it's said, is just results minus expectations.[4]

I think of that phrase "generating wealth and generating envy," and the picture that comes to mind is a scene from *Indiana Jones and the Temple of Doom*, where the floor and ceiling are closing in on him. Above, you have the need to generate wealth, and the floor rising up is envy ... both getting closer and closer, with me in the middle about to get crushed.

So how can I be on social media and also manage those expectations? How can I love my own life and not envy the lives of those around me? I honestly wish there were a magic bullet to make this easier, but unfortunately, I think it is part of the human condition. But we don't have to throw our hands up in the air in defeat; we are stronger than that. We have the capacity to do better, to find contentment in what is.

When I look back on my life, I can see that there is greater happiness to be found in living off less and giving away more than there is in accumulating wealth simply to consume it all personally. There is good that comes from not buying anything you want at any given time. Dare I say it makes you more happy, more grateful, when you do finally get something you waited for. The value of the item increases in the waiting and wanting; our currency gains value again. I think when we decide not to move the goalposts, we push ourselves toward loving the life we have right now. The life right in front of us. And at the same time, when we do get things, we enjoy them all the more because their value has increased.

One of my favorite quotes by Shauna Niequist reads,

> I'm learning, slowly, a rhythm of feasting and fasting that brings a rich cadence to my year. I use the word *fasting* loosely, as an opposite term to *feasting*—permission and discipline, necessary slides back and forth along the continuum of how we feed ourselves.
>
> The weeks between Thanksgiving and New Year's Day are a feast. I love the traditions and tastes of the season—sweet potato biscuits with maple butter, Aunt Mary's raisin bread, toasted and topped with melting sharp cheddar slices.
>
> And then in January, fasting gives me a chance to practice the discipline of not having what I want at every moment, of limiting my consumption, making space in my body and spirit for a new year, one that's not driven by my mouth, by wanting, by consuming.
>
> Fasting, I find, starts as a physical act, but it quickly becomes spiritual: Am I slave to my appetites? Am I ruled by my hunger? Do I trust that God meets my needs, or am I impatient and ravenous, needing to meet them all myself? The rhythm of flavor and feast and celebration during the holidays, tempered by limitations and structure in the new year, draws me closer to God, more dependent, more connected, more grateful for his presence.[5]

I think you can very easily substitute money for food in this text. We can practice the discipline of not having what we want at every moment, of not hitting the Buy Now button on Amazon the moment someone posts a link. We can live a life that isn't driven by wanting and consuming, and in so doing, I think we can find a deeper joy, a more lasting contentment. I cannot tell you how many times I have clicked Buy Now with the hopes that the item that comes will all of a sudden make me cooler. Countless items hang in my closet, rarely worn, because I saw someone pretty wearing them and I thought the items would make me feel pretty. I have wasted so much money in an effort to figure out who I am, stupid enough to think a new shirt could give me the answer.

I do wonder if many of us are actually more content than we even realize. That so much of what we think we want is more a giving in to what the world says should matter. A nicer, bigger, better fill in the blank. I wonder, if we really stepped back, if we would see that the life we have is one filled with extreme happiness and the sacrifices to get more money would not equal the increase in joy we expect to come.

I am still unsure what I will do about the car I wrote about at the beginning of this chapter, but I know in the end it's not really about the car at all. Money never really is about the item itself. But the more I think about our life and our values and where we want the goalpost to stay, the less power I want money and what it represents to have a hold on me. I am realizing that the more I fight to enjoy the current house, or jeans, or family trip, the less I feel a desire for a nicer one. What I have is actually enough.

> **MINDSET SHIFT:** I will not allow the spending or decisions of others to move my goalposts. When I have clearly defined parameters for what matters to me, I can spend money wisely, while also realizing money is not the key to happiness.

MAKING IT PRACTICAL

1. Take some time to really think about your life and the goalposts you have in place. Have they moved significantly over the last few years, and if so, how do you feel about it? (Note: Moving

goalposts is not always a bad thing! However, it's important to notice if they are moving without you even being aware of the change or to keep up with others around you.)

2. Creating a budget and sticking to it can be a powerful way to not only save money but also increase the value of the money you have. When you are forced to say no to certain things you desire, they become more valuable, and if you do finally purchase them, they likely bring more happiness because you had to wait to get them.

3. Consider doing a spending fast, or even just an Amazon fast. Add things to your cart, but do not purchase them for a month. At the end of the month, go and look at the cart and see what items you don't actually want or need.

4. Next time you want to purchase something, pause and ask yourself why. It is absolutely ok if the answer is simply because you want the item, but take a moment to dig a little deeper. Are you trying to keep up with a certain group or trend?

5. Take some time to reflect on your own upbringing. How have the decisions your parents made surrounding finances affected how you think about money? (Were they spenders or savers? Was money a positive topic or stressful one?) If you are married, how is this different from your spouse's upbringing?

CHAPTER 7

I Just Wish I Had More Time

What is this life if, full of care,
We have no time to stand and stare.

No time to stand beneath the boughs
And stare as long as sheep or cows.

No time to see, when woods we pass,
Where squirrels hide their nuts in grass.

No time to see, in broad daylight,
Streams full of stars, like skies at night.

No time to turn at Beauty's glance,
And watch her feet, how they can dance.

No time to wait till her mouth can
Enrich that smile her eyes began.

A poor life this if, full of care,
We have no time to stand and stare.
—William Henry Davies, "Leisure"

Someone asked me recently what was my biggest regret in life. . . .

> "Being in a hurry. Getting to the next thing without fully entering the thing in front of me. I cannot think of a single advantage I've ever gained from being in a hurry. But a thousand broken and missed things, tens of thousands, lie in the wake of all that rushing."
>
> Through all that haste, I thought I was making up time. It turns out I was throwing it away.
>
> —Mark Buchanan, *The Rest of God*

One of my deepest fears is that I will look back in twenty years and realize I didn't use my time well. This is followed closely by the fear that my children would say I didn't have time for them, that I was always too busy. That I would look back and realize I wasted the one precious resource of my one precious life. We all know the saying "We all have the same twenty-four hours in a day." This simple line seems to put us all on the same playing field, as if we really do have the exact same options for how our time will be spent. Of course, this is not the case. There's a myriad of other factors that play into what one can do with their time. Being born into poverty and digging oneself out with countless hours working a minimum wage job does not lend the same amount of free time as someone with ample resources and a savings account. There are a million factors affecting our time, and a million things jockeying for it. This free resource feels anything but.

While Annie Dillard's famous quote saying "How we spend our days is, of course, how we spend our lives"[1] can be helpful, it also haunts me. This quote is a reminder that what I choose to do each moment strings together to form hours. Hours form days, days form weeks, and so on. Before you know it, a decade has passed. But for me, the days would pass, and I would wonder what the heck I even did with the time. Did anything I accomplished add to how I want to spend my life? In her poem "The Summer Day," Mary Oliver writes,

> I do know how to pay attention, how to fall down
> into the grass, how to kneel down in the grass,
> how to be idle and blessed, how to stroll through the fields,
> which is what I have been doing all day.
> Tell me, what else should I have done?
> Doesn't everything die at last, and too soon?
> Tell me, what is it you plan to do
> with your one wild and precious life?[2]

I love this poem. And yet I feel quite different from Mary. I need to meal prep and fold the laundry and wash the high chair tray for the tenth time. I want to be available. Really, I do. I want to have time for others. But there are dishes to do and floors to vacuum and field trip forms to sign. There's too much to do in a day to allow for staring; I do not have the luxury of the sheep and cows Davies writes about.

I have always considered myself to be an efficient and high-energy person. I can get a lot done in a day with my cocker spaniel energy and ability to multitask. This is my superpower. I habit stack like a ninja. I wake up around the same time every morning, exercise, drink my green drink, make a decaf coffee, help the kids with breakfast and getting ready for school, and then eat an English muffin with peanut butter on it. This all happens by 8 a.m., and you could set a clock based on when each of these events occur. I am a machine. In many ways, this level of discipline has served as a necessary way to harness and tame my scattered brain and high energy. The more I can commit to habit, the less space it takes up in my already frazzled mind. Multiple friends have commented on my discipline, usually wishing they had the willpower to do the same. By all outward appearances, this level of efficiency is to be applauded. But deep down, I have wondered if so much of what makes me tick has also made me hard. I might be the person you want to call to help in a crisis, but am I the one you call when you need a hug? These patterns are so ingrained in me that I can have a difficult time pivoting when they get thrown off balance. While I love spontaneity, I want it on my terms. I would not call myself interruptible.

The ability to get a lot done meant I could pack a ton into one day. I would rush from household tasks to something for Naptime Kitchen to prepping dinner to filming content, leaving little to no margin. Busyness was my drug of choice, and at the end of the day I could lay my head on the pillow knowing I got stuff done. This served me well for years—until it didn't. I started to burn out every few weeks. I would have a good cry session, sleep in, then dust myself off and get back to the grind. This pattern went on for months that turned into years. Work a ton, be tired, have a meltdown, crash, wake up and start over.

When John Robert and Scout were toddlers I felt like I had all the time in the world and nothing to fill it with. I bought a new calendar in January, and gloom set in as I realized I had nothing whatsoever to put on it. We spent our mornings surveying different parks or perusing the aisles of Target. I wouldn't have imagined doing online grocery delivery because that would have taken away one of the few precious to-dos on my calendar. The grocery list and meal plan felt like a beacon of hope, a purpose for me on those long days.

I do not say this to demean the tasks of the stay-at-home mom. We had clean clothes because I washed them and food to eat because I shopped for it. Our home ran smoothly because I made it so. But at the end of the day, I couldn't check off a bunch of boxes for accomplished tasks. No one was there handing out a gold star for my kids' lunches. So, I started to cope by keeping us busy. I felt like if we weren't bored then I could at least feel like we were doing things. I would rush us from the park to the kitchen for lunch to playtime to naps, then back to another park to dinner to baths to books to bedtime. I was like the contestants on *Supermarket Sweep*, frantically running around the store shoving things into my cart, slamming into walls as I raced to the register.

I am sad to say life really might have stayed this way till the kids graduated from college if not for the 2020 pandemic. The world completely shut down and with it, so many of the activities I was using to fill our time. The children's museum was closed, along with the aquarium. No one was going to the park; there were no more leisure trips strolling the grocery aisles. We were all home all the time. We even created a makeshift office for Nate in the laundry room, and I remember getting so frustrated when he would stop the dryer to take a work call and forget to start it up again. Time was at a standstill, but Nate still had to work, and I still had around thirteen hours a day with three small humans.

The halt to daily life as we knew it acted as emergency brakes for the freight train I had my kids on. We started to slow down, and it was in that season that I adopted the phrase "Nothing but time." Every day, I would say it over and over and over to myself. Did John Robert want to stop and linger by a pile of rocks on our morning walk? Go for it, buddy, *we got nothin' but time*. Did Scout want another book before naptime? Why not? *We got nothin' but time*. This saying became a balm for my hurried soul. Hourly, I reminded myself we had all the time in the world, and I started to see how much my kids enjoyed the slower pace. They colored longer when I gave them more time to do so. They were more prone to want to go on a walk when I gave them the space to stop and pick a flower.

Eventually, the world began to open back up and with it all the activities and plans. As Naptime Kitchen grew, the earning opportunities did as well, and by the time our third child, Millie, was one, we were a double income family. A lot of the financial stresses we once had were gone, but we were poor in another area: time. Our quality of life felt depleted and unsustainable. The kids were getting older, and we added Alberta to the mix. I remember looking at Nate when Alberta was around a month old and telling him I did not understand why we were both making money if it meant living the way we were. While I had the same amount of time, I had double the demands on my time. John Robert and Scout would want to play a card game at the very same moment Millie needed a diaper change and Alberta was screaming in her crib refusing to nap. And that didn't include all the household demands. Opportunities for Naptime Kitchen were beginning to pick up even more, and Nate still worked long hours as an attorney. He and I felt like ships in the night, each answering the call of kids and work and giving each other what little we had left over at the end of long days.

We both felt stretched to the point of snapping. Nate agreed, and we started thinking through what it would look like if Nate came and started working with me on the backend needs for Naptime Kitchen. He crunched the numbers, and we talked with trusted friends and parents. On paper, we fully expected to lose money. But living on budget was something we perfected in those newly-wed days, and the risk felt worth it. The trade-off of budgeting a bit more for a better quality of life felt like a winning lottery ticket compared to continuing the path we were on. In May of 2022, six months after that initial conversation, Nate left his job.

To many, this looked crazy. Why would we ever trade the financial gains of two incomes? Also, why would Nate leave his secure, consistent job with benefits to come and work with me? In the end, it was simple: time. Nate's job was more consistent and structured, but it also came with more expectations on when and where he worked. While working with me felt more risky, it also allowed us to have more say on how the days were spent. We got to be the boss of our time, and that felt like a bonus bigger than any monetary gain.

This was incredible for our family, but unfortunately, it didn't solve the issue. You see, I am addicted to busyness. If you give someone who loves being busy more time, they will fill it. I was a vacuum, sucking up all the hours I now had with random tasks or projects or errands. I was stressed out and constantly complaining about all I "had to do." I remember on one occasion seeing Nate outside reading a book of poetry and feeling both despondent and jealous. Jealous because I wanted to be reading the book of poetry, and despondent because I knew even if I had the time, I would never sit down to read it.

Because for so many years his time was not his own, Nate had a very different outlook on how he spent his days. Prior to leaving his job there was little time for reading. As an attorney, he charged based on time. He had billable hours to hit, and bonuses if he went beyond those hours. Time was, quite literally, money. Most nights he would stay up late drinking a bourbon, eating chips, and watching TV. I remember him being tired and my suggesting he go to sleep earlier, and his response was so indicative of how he felt: He said 8 p.m. to 10 p.m. felt like the only hours of the day that were truly his. He woke up, helped get the kids ready, got himself ready, worked a full day, came home to supper and bedtime duties, and then, finally, at 8 p.m., he could do something just for him. He said if he didn't stay up late, the next day would start just like the prior, leaving no time for anything he enjoyed. Those two precious hours at night were his saving grace.

He made good money but was not free to take days off when he wanted. Over time, he began to see the freedom of how you spend your time to be the greatest flex and richest resource. Give him two options, one of working himself to the bone living on his own private island, and the other leisurely reading the paper in a moderate house in a normal neighborhood, and he would pick the latter every single time. Nate sees the ability to sit down to read a book for pleasure as the ultimate freedom. Where I see a full to-do list as an identity, he sees it as a burden. Where I see time as something to use up, he sees it as a precious resource.

Luckily, we are married. And at some point, Nate intervened. I do not remember what he said, but the sentiment was that he didn't leave his job to come work with me in order for me to lead a more stressful life. He asked what needed to happen for me to stop feeling the way I was feeling. The answer was not rocket science. I just had to physically make a point to slow down my life. Easy, right? Unfortunately not for someone addicted to the hustle. While I am not an alcoholic, I would imagine the feeling of stillness for a person addicted to being busy might be similar to the feeling of someone addicted to alcohol sitting in a bar. Your fingers start to twitch, your mouth waters. You feel restless and irritable and alone in your thoughts. A small taste of what you long for would help. Just one drink. Just one extra item or errand on the calendar.

You see, I complained about all I had to do, but I loved all I had to do. It had become a defining characteristic of who I was as a person. I didn't know who I was in the stillness, and to be honest, I was a bit afraid of what I might find. *What if I am uninteresting apart from what I accomplish in the day? What if once I stop doing things for people, they don't really love who I am?* These might sound silly, but for those of us who consider ourselves an enneagram three, who we are outside of how we can perform is terrifying.

Yet I knew my marriage and my children were going to suffer if I didn't at least try. And so, in the summer of 2023, I decided to take a month off from posting online and attempt to recalibrate my life. To the outside world it appeared as though I was simply taking a summer month to enjoy my family and vacation. But Nate and I both knew I needed time away from "the internet machine," from the compulsion to pick up my phone and see how people were responding to my latest story or post, from the impulse to film everything I thought would be helpful to share.

We knew we would take a financial loss that month, but it felt necessary. I needed to change the pace of my life, slowly applying the brake pedal to come to a more sustainable speed. And it was not going to happen quickly. The same way I didn't crash and burn overnight, I wasn't going to be fixed in a day. This would be slow and steady. Like a ship with a hole that unloads crate by crate to try to lighten the load, each crate tossed overboard bringing the hull up—inch by inch—until the fear of sinking subsides.

One particular area I knew efficiency had started to take over was in cooking. Taste was no longer the top priority; I wanted speed and ease. I needed simple and oftentimes ready-made. To be fair, I also had four young children. Long laborious meals were not really in the cards, and they weren't going to eat 90 percent of it anyway. But cooking was also the area where I used to come the most alive. The kitchen was the place I felt the most like myself. I knew this was something I came by honestly. Almost every memory I have of my own mom involved her in the kitchen. Each time I drove home from college, I would find her there, apron adorned, stirring or chopping something with the Food Network on in the background. This love for food and cooking was in my blood, but that love had leached out of me.

I started July by ordering two new cookbooks. The first was *Take It Easy* by Gaby Dalkin, and the second was *The Comfortable Kitchen* by Alex Snodgrass. When they arrived, I took a special trip to Office Depot and bought some new sticky tabs and sat on my back porch reading, marking any recipe that looked good with a little tab. I found myself so energized as I flipped through the pages, tabbing recipe after recipe. And there it was in Dalkin's cookbook: a homemade Nutella pie. Complete with homemade Oreo crust and fresh whipped cream. I was in love.

That very weekend I bought what was needed and set to making the pie. When I went to the grocery store, I looked for the premade Oreo pie crust (why make it if I don't have to? Oh, Kate . . . we still had a ways to go), and I am so thankful they didn't have it. Making this pie crust required me to get down the food processor I rarely used and crush up actual Oreos. I counted out the twenty-five cookies the recipe called for, stuck them in the processor with the melted butter, and pushed the button. The Oreos were pulverized to the most perfect sand-like consistency, with the addition of the butter making it slightly sticky. I used my hands to press the mixture into my pie crust and stuck this into the oven to bake for seven minutes. While it cooked, I got to work on the filling. First, whipping the cream. It had been years since I had made homemade whipped cream, and I forgot just how lovely it is. The way you have to watch it closely, making sure you whip it enough so that you don't have soup and not so much that you get butter. This recipe called for soft peaks, and I enjoyed showing the kids the difference between a soft peak and a stiff one. I divided the whipped cream, setting half aside for topping, and got to work on the cream cheese and Nutella.

Using a hand mixer on a block of cream cheese and Nutella is not for the faint of heart, but after a minute or so you start to get this absolutely decadent, thick, milky-creamy-cheesy-chocolate filling. And then you get to do the very best part: You add half of that fresh whipped cream in and watch that thick, cheesy chocolate become light and silky smooth. You have to wait for your pie shell to cool, and then you pour the Nutella filling inside. And here's the hardest part: It then needs to go into the fridge to set.

I do not have the cookbook in front of me, yet I can recount every step in making the pie. It required my full attention and patience to wait between the steps. This wasn't break and bake cookie dough. This was slow, purposeful work. This was measuring and waiting and cooling and filling. And what came of that work was nothing short of absolutely delicious. I shared the pie with my family and then kept the final few slices for myself. Each afternoon I would cut a slice, top it with homemade whipped cream, and sit on the back porch to enjoy. Because of the effort it took to make this pie, I found myself wanting to savor the experience of eating it. Everything about it from start to finish was glorious.

For years I had scoffed at people who made homemade pasta. Why would they waste all that time and energy when ready-made is available? I get it now. This is not wasted time. There is something being restored inside a person when they make something from start to finish. Whether it's a bookshelf or soufflé, there's an art to it that touches at a piece of who I am as a human. I was made by a Creator and have an innate desire to create. But I let myself become too busy for it. I microwave and get grocery delivery and buy items preassembled. None of those things are bad, but with my life catapulting toward burnout, I was deeply in need of a change. And the most basic, practical way I saw myself starting was by trading boxed soup for a slow stew. Not every night, but more often. To force myself to allow for more margin and time.

I wish I could say that summer healed me, but I am learning this propulsion to always be doing more, more, more is a part of my identity. My hands are clenched around that to-do list so tightly that you literally have to pry one finger at a time to get me to let it go. This goes for how our home runs as well. For years, I didn't really want Nate to bring me flowers. Not because I didn't like flowers, but because our house felt chaotic enough, and I didn't want another thing to care for or find a place for. In the summer, our neighbors have an incredible garden, and the kids are constantly bringing foliage into the house to proudly display in a mason jar on the kitchen table. Much like the Nutella pie, flowers push at another pain point and challenge me to let go and simply be. Our house does not have to have pristine surfaces to function well. No one is performing surgery on our countertops. But when you are moving fast, there's no room for excess trinkets. I was the bull in the china shop, so I made a home without any china in it. I am slowly training my heart to let the warmth in, the stems and vases, the excess items that allow my children to feel safe. Strangely, as I do so, I am feeling my heart rate slow. My home feels familiar and lived in. I feel more ok in who I am and the time I am allotted, more comfortable to not get it all done. To miss out on things and let the carpet be dirty one more day. Some days it is easy, and others it feels like the most painful of surgeries.

As I started to slow down, I noticed that everyone around me was also feeling a general need to rush and get things done. This is nothing new. Books like *The Ruthless Elimination of Hurry* and *Chasing Slow* weren't written for no one. Our culture loves hurry, yet we also long to be still. We love the idea of the poetry book, but we don't really want to sit down and read it. All of my friends, from those who homeschool to those whose kids are in school to those who work to those who don't, would still say they feel really busy—and with so many good things like children and church and extracurriculars and friendships. Life can be really, really full of good things, but I also think far too many of us are stuffing our calendars, so rushed we can barely enjoy what's in front of us. Overwhelmed by the calendar and at the same time underwhelmed with life.

So what do we do to gain time? We can't just not work or eat or live in filth. But I don't really think that's what any of us are craving anyway. Everyone loves a vacation, but after a week or so you start to feel stale. You begin to itch for a little routine and consistency; you crave a walk and a salad. We like having things to do and feeling like we are using the time well; we just want a little margin. Margin, to me, is small slivers of vacation sprinkled into our everyday lives. Too much margin and you can feel bored or antsy, too little margin and you feel tired and frantic. I wish this was an easy balance to strike, but sometimes it takes a season of too much busyness to realize you need space to breathe, a season of treading water to realize you were close to drowning.

While the decisions made around how to spend time can be difficult, I do think a mental shift helped me win back my days. That shift came in seeing time as a precious resource rather than an abundant one. Currency holds weight because it is meant to be backed by gold. When more and more paper money is printed, it cheapens the value of all money because the paper is no longer backed by anything of tangible value. Print too much money, and all money loses value. Time is funny; it isn't something you can print more of like money, yet it renews daily. It renews daily and is, at the same time, a limited resource. Because it renews daily, it is something we can continuously learn from. We are each presented with the same twenty-four hours every morning until we die, and some days we will use the hours much better than others.

There are so many demands on our time that we have no control over, but I think many of us have more agency than we realize. Every single decision you make has a cost, and it is up to you to decide if the cost is worth it. As you start to value your time more, you can see what activities feel enjoyable and worth the cost of time, and what things are draining and likewise not worth the higher cost. To be clear, I do not do this perfectly, and it's oftentimes only in hindsight that I can see where a certain cost on my time was not a good one. But like I said, time renews daily, and I can continually be learning.

Most of the demands are the same as before. There's still laundry and dishes and extracurriculars. We still go from the park to dinner to bedtime. But there's more purpose, more fullness, in these activities now. I have started asking how I can better enjoy the daily required tasks, and how I can create more margin for the things I do enjoy. I have found it almost always comes back to saying no more often—to valuing my time and what I spend it on. Am I less social now? Probably. But the depth and quality of where I give my time feels better than it has in years.

That last sentence feels iffy, because by the time you read this I could be in another tailspin, frantically filling my days with senseless things. Let's just say I am in rehab. But time means more to me than it used to, and while I can't actually get more of it, I will fight like crazy to savor how I spend it. Like a sweet piece of homemade pie.

> **MINDSET SHIFT:** While I can't get time back, I can learn from it. Time is free, yet it also has a cost, and each day I can become a bit wiser in how I choose to spend it.

·········· MAKING IT PRACTICAL ··········

1. I think one of the most valuable things we can do is start to see time as a valued, life-giving resource instead of something to simply fill. I know few have time for homemade pasta every day, but I do believe these (on the surface) superfluous acts are doing something much deeper for our souls. What is an activity you have wanted to try but scoff at the time it takes? What would you have to give up to make it happen?

2. I have started to focus on how I spend a period of time as opposed to what I got done in that time. This might be a small shift, but it's had some profound benefits. For example, I am focusing simply on reading before bed and not on keeping a running list of how many books I can get through. I am reading simply for the sake of reading, not for any achievement I can get from it. Reading is for the sole purpose of enjoying that time. Do you have hobbies like this that you could enjoy simply for the purpose of doing and not for the end result?

3. Get a sheet of paper and write down all the things asking for your time. Then, categorize them as necessary or optional tasks. (Note: necessities are things like work, sleep, school, ordering groceries, etc. While your child's soccer practice might feel like a necessity, it is optional. More on this in point 4.) Take stock of this list and rate what gives the most life to your family

versus what is the most draining. There are definitely going to be some draining things that have to stay, but there might be a few that could be dropped. If you are rich in other areas and poor in time, consider an area you could hire out help to some capacity.

4. If you have children, helping them learn to value their own time matters. It could be that they are overextended, burned out, and need a parent to help them pump the brakes. Maybe soccer has become something they are passionate about and want to commit to, and they need to let go of something else to have the margin and energy to do soccer well. You could do the same exercise in number three with your child to help them see what they are giving their time to. (Unfortunately, a large part will likely be school, and they might happily tell you they are happy to cut that one out.) As you teach your child about time, you help them learn to value it.

5. In the words of Peter Drucker, "There is surely nothing quite so useless as doing with great efficiency what should not be done at all."[3] Are there things you are fighting like crazy to make work in your schedule which really should not be done at all? Are there tasks you put on yourself which no one is asking of you?

CHAPTER 8

I Just Wish I Had Control

> Of course it is happening inside your head, Harry, but why on earth should that mean that it is not real?
> —J.K. Rowling, *Harry Potter and the Deathly Hallows*

My uncle died in a car accident one week before I left for my freshman year of college. He had flown down to Florida to purchase a used Porsche and was driving it up I-95 back to South Carolina. We actually talked on the phone that day as he was driving back and made plans for him to take me out to a fancy restaurant the following Tuesday to celebrate my leaving for college. I had just broken up with my longtime high school boyfriend, and "Dog Dog," as we called him, asked me for the details. I kept it pretty short on the phone and told him I would fill him in at dinner. There was a typical August-afternoon thunderstorm, and sometime in the following hours he hydroplaned and hit a tree.

I remember exactly where I was and how my mom told me he had died. I remember the grief on her face having just lost her brother, and the deeper grief in hearing her talking to my cousins on the phone, who at ages twenty and fourteen had just lost their father.

My grandparents were out of town at the time, celebrating their anniversary in Maine. My mom and her sister Ellen flew up to tell them what had happened. When I asked my mom to make sure I had the details right, she said she can remember every moment of that day. More than anything, she remembered the huge smile on my grandfather's face, thinking his kids were there as some sort of anniversary surprise. The devastation surrounding that situation was so tangible I can still feel it in my stomach. My grandparents lost their son, my mom lost her brother, and my cousins lost their dad. And then, less than ten years later, those same two cousins lost their mother. It seemed as though the grief and loss were being piled on them in giant bulldozer-sized scoops.

A neighbor down the street lost their four-year-old to cancer last year. Were he alive, he would be the same age as Millie. They have four kids just like us, and when I see their family on walks, there is this gap where you know their second-born child should be. My friend Maggie's mom, Nan, got diagnosed with brain cancer, and Maggie found out on the exact day she was throwing me my very first wedding shower. Nan would die a few years later, cancer robbing her of time to come with her grandchildren, and robbing Maggie of her mother in those early postpartum years when you long for a mother's help the most. You really don't live very long before you start to know people who have lived through absolutely awful tragedy. Crashes and cancer diagnoses and heart failures come, leaving those left behind with broken hearts of their own. And this is in America, arguably one of the safest, most medically advanced countries in the world.

In contrast, my life has been really, really wonderful. Aside from my uncle's passing, no huge tragedy has struck me personally. Nate lost his dad suddenly in 2020, and watching him go through that was awful, but I have not personally had something strike me in that same manner. Most would call me lucky, and I am. But it has also left me in a constant state of waiting for something terrible to happen, fearing some tragedy is lurking just around the corner. Life can't possibly be this good forever.

There was a popular sermon series during my college years where the pastor was making the point that bad things are going to happen to everyone in life. It was couched under a greater theme that all of life is suffering, and we shouldn't be surprised when the hard times come. God is not punishing you; He is there for you in those hard moments and loves you. This was meant to be good news. Unfortunately, what those pastors didn't know was that I was the last person who needed to be reminded that suffering happens; my anxiety had me searching for it around every corner.

What this belief ended up doing was making someone who had an amazing life they should be grateful for begin to hole up in fear. Just like the pastor said: Bad things were coming for me at some point. Instead of living in joy and gratitude, I crouched down in fear, eyes darting to try to catch the proverbial shoe when it dropped.

My anxiety was peaking around the time Nate and I started seriously dating, and my biggest fear at that time was losing him to some tragedy. I kid you not, when Nate was flying home from Asia, my father gave me a Xanax to calm me down. Me, feet firmly planted in the soil, needed a Xanax for the plane ride Nate was on.

And that's the crappy thing about control: There are too many situations to have a handle on them all. I couldn't control Nate's airplane over the Indian Ocean any more than I could control the speed and rainfall that night my uncle drove down the interstate.

I wish I could tell you that it got better after this realization, but children only brought more areas for concern. And so I took the path of least resistance to the emotion I knew best: anxiety.

I would borrow worry and stick it deep down in my pocket like a pretty shell I found at the beach. I would put my hand in my pocket and feel its shape. I memorized its every groove and crevice, thinking that if I came to know the worry enough, live it enough, then my heart would be prepared if such tragedy should ever come.

This is irrational on so many fronts. First off, the notion that worrying about a tragedy will deter a tragedy is futile. Like Van Wilder's rocking chair analogy says, worrying gave me something to do, but it didn't get me anywhere.[1] Second, I was putting my body through emotions it had no reason to be feeling. Like putting myself through vigorous drills for a sport I do not even play, I was an Olympic athlete in anxiety, and the training was grueling.

But you know what fear doesn't care about? Rational thoughts.

I had a friend tell me they recently heard of an awful story where a family was hiking in California, and a mountain lion took their toddler who had run ahead on the path. Yep, just jumped out and took the child. Poof. I did some research online and never found the story. There were some attacks, but no mountain lion child abductions that I could find. It should also be noted I live in Charleston. There has not been a confirmed cougar or mountain lion sighting in the state of South Carolina for over one hundred years. But you know what new fear I activated? An animal taking my child while we are out hiking. All from a third-hand story I was never able to get any proof actually occurred. But just like fear doesn't care about being rational, it also doesn't really care if it's happened to you. All it needs is a tiny foothold in your brain to take root and begin to grow.

We have had some near misses hit closer to home. In the summer of 2021, there was a terrifying instance involving Millie and a pool. It was exactly the type of scenario that haunts your dreams as a parent, a too-close call that woke me multiple times a night over the following weeks, replaying what happened. We were all right there! We thought we had eyes on her. And yet, how easily she slipped below the surface, quiet as a mouse; the hot asphalt on my bare feet as I sprinted toward her; seeing her body suspended in water, desperate eyes looking up at me, mouth gasping for air; holding her to my body, thanking God over and over. *It could have been so much worse.*

Similarly, Nate was in a terrible car wreck a few years back that very well could have killed him. He was driving home over the Cooper River Bridge in five o'clock traffic and was cut off by another car. This caused him to slam on the brakes and spin out of control, his car doing a full one-eighty before it slammed into the guardrail of the bridge. Nate, sitting in his totaled car, was now facing the onslaught of oncoming traffic during the busiest time of day. By some miracle, there wasn't a car in the lane next to him when this happened, and the oncoming traffic had enough time to stop before hitting him.

I left the kids with a neighbor and raced toward the bridge. Since he was in the lanes that come toward downtown, I had to cross the entire way over the bridge northbound and then re-enter it going southbound in order to get to him. The Cooper River Bridge is massive, spanning three miles across the Charleston Harbor. I was only halfway across, and I could already see the ambulances, fire trucks, and police cars on the other side. A cacophony of lights and people and cars stopped as far as the eye could see, so many likely annoyed to be stuck in traffic from the accident. And me, knowing my husband was that accident. But I knew he was ok. I had talked to him. *It could have been so much worse.*

There was a Sunday afternoon years ago, when we were living in Durham, where it had been raining for what felt like weeks. It finally started to let up, and people poked their heads from their houses like hermit crabs from shells, so happy to see the sunshine. I was doing the usual Sunday chores, putting a load in the laundry and grabbing fresh bed sheets, when a message came through to our neighborhood group text from my friend Jessica: "Does anyone know a little boy named Theo? Around nine years old. He was just hit by a car up by the stop sign on Cornwallis." There was only one Theo in the neighborhood that I could recall, and he was nine. His little sister had been in the nursery with John Robert. I knew his mom, Stacy. I ran out to tell Nate, then got in my car to drive up to the stop sign on Cornwallis. I didn't know what I was going to do, only that I knew who he was and could help with any questions they had if they weren't yet in touch with Stacy.

When I arrived there were five police cars and an ambulance. I wondered if this was what the scene looked like in Florida the afternoon my uncle died. I was sitting in my car when I saw Stacy speed onto the street, eyes white with fear. Luckily, Theo was fine. His bike was totaled, but he miraculously walked away from the accident with little more than a scraped knee. *It could have been so much worse.*

John Robert is currently eight, and I am starting to see a desire in him for some independence. He can ride a bike very well. He can swim. He has my phone number memorized. Heck, he even has a GPS watch. He has shown me in so many areas that he is responsible and trustworthy. And yet, I still struggle with letting him go out on his own. I see kids his age riding their bikes and not looking both ways or swerving as they ride, and I get nervous. What if they aren't looking, and a car hits them? What if the next message on my new neighborhood group text has to do with another child on a bike, and that child is my son?

We have been playing a lot of Monopoly Deal as a family, and while there is some skill involved, like many card games, it is largely a game of luck. Sometimes we will be midgame, Nate clearly in the lead, and there's one or two cards he needs to draw to win. He is playing smart, making good decisions, but simply can't get the card he needs. Scout plays a bit more recklessly. She gets excited and lays cards quickly; she thinks only about that one turn and not future moves. In a game, Nate can do everything right and never draw the card he needs, while Scout can play recklessly and end up getting a lucky draw to win the game.

Scout could win the game and be led to believe she's a really good player, when all she had was some good luck. Likewise, Nate could think he is a bad card player when he was simply dealt a bad hand. Former pro poker player Annie Duke calls this "resulting." In short, if you're judging the quality of a decision from afar, you often judge the decision based on results. If it's a bad outcome, you assume it was a bad decision. On the flip side, sometimes you can make every right decision and have bad luck. We ignore how much luck plays a role in the equation. The same way you can't believe you are awesome simply because you had a good outcome, you also can't believe you are a terrible person because you had a bad outcome.[2] Nate isn't a bad card player because he lost the game any more than Stacy is a bad mom because her son was in an accident.

There are so many near misses in life, so many almosts and could-have-been-worses. Legitimate opportunities for me to wring my hands in worry. But I have to choose to fight for the bigger, better outcome: a life we love and get to enjoy. How will Millie learn to swim if we don't allow her in the water? How will John Robert learn to ride his bike to school if we don't allow him to start with a loop around the block? How will Nate drive to work if he doesn't get back behind the wheel?

But the struggle with anxiety and how to deal with it continues. I hear of the "good old days" when my parents rode their bikes without helmets and came home at dark. There were no fancy watches or cell phones to check in; there was just a general trust they were with their friends and would be home for supper. I am fairly certain my dad was driving a johnboat around the Charleston harbor at age eight, and I am guessing life jackets weren't required.

In one dinnertime conversation, my dad can reminisce about these good old days, and by dessert someone has shared three awful stories they read online. A child who drowned, a ten-car pileup on the interstate, and a teen saved from an awful sex predator online are all discussed over warm brownies and ice cream. Technology has given us so many stories at our fingertips, opportunity after opportunity to read something and absorb a new fear deep into our bones. We have become more street smart and at the same time more scared to let our children play on the neighborhood street.

The area in life where I struggle the most with anxiety and control is undoubtedly travel. I do not love to travel. Actually, that's not true. I love to visit new and exciting places, to see new cultures and taste new foods. I love to immerse myself in a world quite different from my own. I just don't love the process of physically getting there. Perhaps, I should say, I love the arrival, but not the journey.

The hardest of all (you guessed it!): air travel. (Remember, I am the one who took a Xanax with my feet firmly planted on American soil while Nate was in the air.)

Stick me in a plane over any large body of water, and I'll likely need medication to stay calm. I am convinced the plane will have a malfunction or there's a terrorist on board. I wish I could say I was joking, but this is my reality. Head darting left to right on the plane, looking for someone with a burner phone (an unfortunate side effect of watching way too much *Homeland*) and saying my end-of-life prayers at the slightest turbulence. Rationally, I know you are safer in a plane than driving a car. And yet, each and every time I got on an airplane, I would believe deep down that it was going to crash. Nate would assure me that a commercial airline hadn't crashed in over a decade, and I would look at him and say in a deadpan tone, "We are about to change that statistic."

In the last ten years, this fear took on a new form: highway travel. And unfortunately, if you want to go just about anywhere new or see anyone you love who isn't nearby, you will likely be met with the option to take a plane or drive a long way on a highway. I wanted to see my friends and not just over FaceTime. I wanted to hug Nate's family in Pennsylvania. I wanted to go on a whale watch in Alaska and take the kids hiking out west. None of these things were going to happen apart from some serious travel.

The last transatlantic flight I took, I was so stressed beforehand that I made an end-of-life video telling the kids how much I loved them and texted it to my friend Molly. (Molly is just anxious enough to not consider me a total weirdo for making said video.)

Nate and I were set to go on a family trip to Italy with my grandmother, sans kids. While anyone looking in would consider this trip a dream vacation, I was an absolute ball of nerves. I made that doomsday goodbye video to send to my children should Nate and I perish and texted it to Molly, and I had a general pit in my stomach whenever I thought about the trip. I was dreading going to Italy! This is not how it should be. A few weeks before we left, we met with our church small group, and during prayer requests I mentioned my anxieties. One of the girls in the group, Maggie, said the simplest line, which turned out to be completely profound to me, and I have thought about it every single time I have flown since.

Maggie jested, "But what if you choose not to go to Italy and instead stay home with your kids? And then, on your way to the aquarium, you get in a car wreck on the exact week you would have been in Italy?" I know her logic might feel morbid, but it was like a switch flipped in my brain. For some reason the sense that I could just as easily die in my car freed me. It made me feel like I couldn't make a decision that would wreck my life; I didn't have that much control. We went to Italy, and I am so grateful, because five months later the pandemic shut the world down.

In January of 2022, after a solid two years of very limited air travel, I knew I needed to get back on the horse. I booked a flight to Florida for a girls' weekend. It might not seem like much, but it was a starting point. And then I booked another flight, and another, each time holding my breath as I clicked *Confirm* on the screen. In the days before each trip, when the email prompting me to check in early came, dread set in, and my nerves were in a ball with each drive to the airport.

Then something very unexpected started to happen. Something was helping me be less fearful when flying on airplanes. Something that, had you suggested it to me a year ago, would have made me laugh in your face. It wasn't a pill or even a prayer.

That something: *flying on airplanes.*

The more I got on airplanes, the less scary airplanes began to feel. The more I safely took off and landed, the easier it was to do it again the next time. I was unknowingly putting myself through exposure therapy. With each repetition, the fear and anxiety dulled. Dare I say I began to enjoy it. I also realized I love airports. I love the hustle and bustle of a million people going to a million different places for a million different reasons. I love that bars are open at 8 a.m., and you can often order a cheeseburger for breakfast. Time moves differently in an airport, and the change of pace was invigorating. Something I feared for so long actually had a lot to offer me; I just had to do it to see it.

Perhaps the reason things like daily car travel don't feel as scary is simply because I do them so often. It's not that driving down the road is any safer (statistics say the opposite), but doing it so much more often dulls the risky feeling. I'm sure I was terrified the first time I took an on-ramp onto the freeway in drivers' ed, but now it's become an everyday activity that no longer causes fear in me. I have a handle on it; I feel in control. I love control. It's like a cozy blanket, making me feel safe and secure.

But in reality, I am no more in control behind the wheel of my own car than I am in the twenty-third row of an aircraft.

I just think I am.

I have this misbelief that as long as I am behind the wheel, as long as I have the kids, as long as I have the power, I can make it ok. "I have got this covered, God! Don't worry about us. I can handle the day-to-day, you just step in for the big things like flights and emergencies."

And this got me thinking more about travel in general. I feel like there's one of two options: I can see how God is again and again sustaining me, or I can begin to get a false sense of control and think I am the one doing it.

I also noticed that when I came home from an airplane trip, I found myself extra thankful to be home—to be there to tuck in my children at bedtime. But if my above argument is true, that I really am no longer in control, then the level of gratitude to see them after a flight shouldn't actually outweigh the gratitude when we drive home from Target on a random Tuesday. The mere repetition just makes it appear less risky. The reps make me think I can do more of it on my own. But I am not doing any of it on my own! And in recognizing that, I realize my trust in God should be ever present in my mind.

He is not just there for the flight. He is there daily as we pack lunches and drive to school. If I see Him in the routine reps, it's easier to see Him in the big moments as well. If I see Him as the one carrying us safely down the street, it makes it easier to see how He carries that aircraft.

As I hopefully continue to fly more, I pray the reps don't give me a false sense of control but rather further reveal the reality that He is in control.

Find my seat, buckle up. Ask God to watch over this flight. *Rep.*

Visualize His hand under the airplane, holding it and guiding it to our destination. *Rep.*

Feel the wheels hit the landing strip. Turn on my phone, and text Nate that I have landed safely. Thank God. *Rep.*

Rep after rep after rep.

But not just on the plane.

Wake up, thank God for another day. *Rep.*

My kids are safely at school and there when I pick them up. God protecting them. *Rep.*

Food in the fridge for dinner. God's provision. *Rep.*

He is, ever and always, in the details.

Here's something beautiful I have come to realize about control: It used to be I only saw control as something that would ward off the bad. In this way, I was missing so many good things that had happened in my life outside of my control. I couldn't control Nate deciding to transfer schools and ending up in North Carolina. I couldn't control the unseasonably warm New Year's Day we had in 2019, when my dad took us all out on the boat and we saw over fifty porpoises, causing the kids to scream in delight. I couldn't control the fact that the car beside Nate was paying really good attention, slamming on their brakes and missing his car the day it spun out on the Cooper River Bridge. There were far more good things happening outside of my control.

Anxiety remains my deepest struggle and the biggest burden I carry. There's a real chance the other shoe will drop, and eventually the people I love will die. But I think my biggest regret would be worrying about events that never came to fruition, wringing my hands over ideations, when right in front of me precious, incredible life is happening. The more good I notice and realize is outside of my control, the easier it gets to loosen the grip I have so tightly on how I believe my life should look. It's like I am holding the painting too close to my eyes, and if I would simply hang it on the wall and step back from it, I could see the larger picture. I could see how all the brush strokes, even the seemingly ugly ones, come together to make something beautiful—if only I would loosen my grip, take a breath, and step back to see it.

MINDSET SHIFT: The biggest way I can conquer my anxiety is to realize I have far less control than I think I do. The good news is that control isn't just about avoiding disasters; so many good things are happening in my life outside of my control too! When I put my focus there, my need for control dissipates. When I let go of the tight grasp on my life, anxiety lets go of its tight grasp on me.

MAKING IT PRACTICAL

1. To begin noticing how the good in your life works beyond your control, I cannot suggest enough doing some form of gratitude journal. Whether you keep a running list on the counter or simply think of three things before you go to sleep, noticing how much good happens outside of your control has an incredible ability to loosen the tight grip you have on your life and those you love.

2. Visualize a photo album. What sort of pictures do you hope will fill it? Are there places or people you hope have a photo in the album? Maybe it's an anniversary trip you want to take or a sport that one of the kids dreams of playing. So many adventures are possible, and it's helpful to remember the bigger dream that makes the risks worth taking.

3. If you do not have a will, I suggest making one. Do this long before you take a trip, because if you try to do it within the same week of your travel, you will have a massive anxiety spike. Ask me how I know! Having one allows me to breathe easier leading up to travel, knowing the big, important decisions that would need to be made should the worst happen have already been made.

4. What spikes my anxiety: caffeine. It catapults me to a breaking point much faster than I would otherwise get there. If this is you, consider lessening or cutting it altogether. What helps my anxiety: exercise. Exercise has been one of the most transformative things I have ever done for my anxiety. I am very high energy and tend to wake up feeling like a kettle near boiling over, and early exercise takes the edge off for me. I used to think exercise was a way I helped my anxiety apart from God, but now I see exercise is a way God allows my body to actively dissipate my anxiety.

5. Back when Nate was in Malaysia and I had to take that Xanax, I remember a conversation I had with my friend Tiffany. Tiffany lived her life with a lightness I longed for. She just didn't seem to wake up with the fear that something bad was going to happen. I asked her, "How can you be so worry-free in life? What are you doing that I am not?" Her response struck me as so obvious and practical I have never forgotten it, and it's been one of the single most helpful pieces of advice I have ever gotten when it comes to worrying for my family. She told me that if one of those things were going to happen, it would be awful, but all the feelings and grief would come then. But how much more awful would it be to live my whole life worrying about these things and then get to eighty and look back at all the things I feared that never happened, all the time and energy wasted on scenarios that never came to fruition? Just like I did with my friend Tiffany, find people in your life who you admire for their lack of fear and anxiety, and ask them about it. Learn from their perspective and wisdom.

CHAPTER
9

I Just Wish My Life Looked More Like Hers

> You may get to the very top of the ladder, and then find it has not been leaning against the right wall.
>
> —Allen Raine

My favorite movie of 2023 was Greta Gerwig's *Barbie*. I went with all the women in the family on my mom's side and left with a stomachache from laughing so hard. It was not at all what I expected in the very best way possible. The movie opens with a utopian world called Barbie Land. Every Barbie is happy and content in who she is. Every Barbie has a role and feels deeply satisfied with how she contributes to society. In one scene, a Nobel Prize is handed out for journalism, and the Barbie who receives it joyfully responds, "I work very hard, so I deserve it," and all the other Barbies cheer emphatically. No one is jealous. Narrator Helen Mirren gives us a snapshot into all that Barbie has accomplished: "She might have started out as just a lady in a bathing suit, but she became so much more. She has her own money, her own house, her own car, her own career."[1] *She has it all.*

There are a few digs in these opening scenes that are extremely important: first, Midge. Midge is Barbie's pregnant friend, and Mirren notes, "Let's not show Midge, actually. She was discontinued by Mattel because a pregnant doll is just too weird."[2] All the Barbies in Barbie Land have careers, but none have the role of being a mother. Come to think of it, none are married or have families at all.

All of this is meant to be satire, but these opening scenes pack so much to think about. First off, there's this world where Barbies have a role and purpose and feel so wonderful about themselves. There's also no comparison or gossip. However, there isn't any death, sadness, or cellulite either. There are also no children or mothers from what we can tell (apologies to Midge, who lives in an eternal state of third trimester misery). No Barbie has stretch marks or a bad night's sleep or the struggle between the demands of home life and personal dreams. The worries in her life are as scarce as the wrinkles on her skin.

Barbie wakes up and does the same sorts of activities every day. In Barbie Land, nobody compares because in large part everyone's life is actually the same. Everyone has a purpose, and everyone feels fulfilled in their purpose. Mail Lady Barbie delivers the mail. Pilot Barbie flies the planes. It's all very simple. Then Stereotypical Barbie (played by Margot Robbie) begins to have strange things happen to her. She has "irrepressible feelings of death," her feet flatten to no longer be in the perfect shape for stilettos, and cellulite begins to form on her legs. She is concerned about these things and told to visit Weird Barbie, who is portrayed perfectly and hilariously by Kate McKinnon. Weird Barbie tells Barbie she is going to have to go to the real world and fix what is happening to her, but Barbie doesn't want to go. Weird Barbie's response is simply, "Fine, get cellulite, I don't care." Barbie screams in disgust, "No! No, no, no. No!"[3] Barbie will risk it all to avoid cellulite.

Social media can feel a bit like Barbie Land. It allows us a place to see the fun side of people's lives while often hiding the harder Weird Barbie side. It allows for a series of pictures and videos highlighting accomplishments and milestones, because that's what we like to see. Who wants to post the picture at the beach where your stretch marks glisten in the sunlight? No, we tuck those away or delete them, reserving the better angles for posting. You don't post the multiple tantrums your child had on the family vacation but rather the photo of them smiling with their goggles and sun hat on. It's a highlight of pleasures without the pain. And I get it; I do it too.

I was looking through photos on my phone and came across one of Scout from our trip to New York City when she was five years old. We ate, we shopped, we soaked up all New York City at Christmas had to offer. We had no responsibilities or obligations. The entire trip was just perfect. But on the final night, Scout spiked a fever and was in bed by 6 p.m. What's interesting is that I really only remembered her getting sick from this one photo, and I only took this photo to send to Nate. It wasn't a trip highlight I wanted to reminisce on. On every trip, I take photos of things I want to remember. I post photos I want to memorialize. I've got rose-colored camera lenses. Rarely do I have a desire to photograph the screaming child, the fight with Nate, the acne, the boring toast I eat every single day. It's not that those things don't exist, they simply aren't what my brain wants to hold on to.

When I am not in a good headspace, I forget and instead think this tiny clip from someone's day encompasses their whole day. I then compare that clip to my not-so-bad very normal day, and all of a sudden, I feel lacking. My ordinary life isn't anything special compared to their awesome day at the beach. I compare the whole of my day to the tiny snapshots of theirs, and I get a skewed view of reality on both sides. My day feels less-than, and theirs appears robust with joy and fun, even if that isn't the case. I cannot compare the pace of someone running a one-hundred-yard dash to the pace of a marathon runner, but that is essentially what I am doing. I take their fifteen seconds and put it beside my fifteen hours. It really makes no sense when I think about it logically, but it's hard to use good logic when I'm sleep-deprived, in desperate need of a shower, and the baby just puked on my shoulder.

But I do wonder if those less glamorous moments are all a part of the larger best life I am hoping for. Creating a family includes baby puke. Running a marathon includes training and blisters and early mornings. Even a perfect day at the beach involves getting sand in my bathing suit.

I have a photo on my desk of me holding Millie in the hospital. She can't be more than twenty-four hours old. She's so tiny and squishy and perfect. I am also squishy. My eyes are swollen from lack of sleep, but also somehow bright. I am wearing hospital grade underwear and a diaper to help with the trauma my body went through to have this baby girl, and yet I am so incredibly happy. I am in so much pain; my hormones are an absolute wreck; I am getting little to no sleep; I have this new creature that completely depends on me; I am overwhelmed; and yet, I am deeply joyful and grateful. I feel cracked open and at the same time whole.

When I first watched that opening scene of Barbie, I wanted it to be true for women everywhere. I wanted to live in Barbie Land! But I quickly realized I could not. I am married, I have a family I love, and I have hopes and dreams outside of Barbie's parameters. The things lacking in Barbie's world are many of the things that give life the most meaning. Arguing with a spouse and swallowing your pride, working daily to make a marriage that lasts. Saying no to many things you want in order to save money for a car. Caring for your parents as they age. Coming home after work, tired and weary, and gearing up for the second shift of dinner, piggyback rides, and bedtime for your toddlers. These small moments of chosen suffering are creating the life you have longed for: the fifty-year wedding anniversary, the road trip, being with your parents, and making a family. Barbie Land, while fun, feels a bit like a perpetual vacation. It's enjoyable, but after a certain amount of time even the beach becomes lackluster. It's like a coffee with too much sugar, saccharinely sweet. Drink too much of it, and you feel sick.

In order to not get caught up in the Barbie Lands of others, I have to know what game I am playing. What I mean by that is I have to decide what matters to me in my life and what goals I am working toward. And the game I play can change over time. When Nate and I were first married we put a lot of effort into saving money in order to get out of law school with as little debt as possible. We made decisions to win that game. When we saw friends go on extravagant vacations or buy a new car, we had to remind ourselves that was not the game we were playing. To do those things would put us in further debt and actually make us lose the game that mattered the most to us.

In the moment, this was not fun for me. I wanted money for clothes and to not be so stringent at the grocery store. I saw people my same age with nicer apartments and cars and taking better vacations, and I was bitter. Whatever game they were playing looked a lot more fun than my own, and I made sure my husband knew it. Looking back, I think this was a hard season for Nate. He had an unhappy wife at home, angry she couldn't buy new trinkets at Target every time the season changed. A wife that made him feel guilty for not making more money. Of course, in the long run, paying for law school over Target trinkets was the right choice, but at the time I was angry, and I took that anger out on him. I didn't have a good handle on what mattered and what we were working toward.

If I don't focus on the game I am playing, I quickly lose sight of what's important to me. I was listening to an interview on *The Lazy Genius* podcast between Kendra Adachi (the host) and James Clear (author of arguably the most popular book on habits of all time, *Atomic Habits*). They were discussing Jerry Seinfeld and his dedication to never miss a day of working on his jokes.[4] Seinfeld has shared publicly that he has been successful at keeping this streak going, and it's impressive! However, you have to wonder what cost it had in other areas of his life. There are things he had to say no to in order to say yes to writing jokes daily. Kendra made the observation that he really wanted to be a famous comedian, and so writing jokes every day in a super strict manner was very important to him, arguably his highest goal. And he did it! He is, after all, Jerry Seinfeld. But he knew the game he was playing, and he dedicated hours to it for years in order to achieve it. There's a ton of hard days and training that happened in the background we never saw, and a lot of games he likely lost. We see the success of his career, not the time away from his friends and family, or opportunities he said no to in order to say yes to honing his craft. He might have been letting balls drop in a million areas, but this is the area that mattered to him—practicing comedy every day was the ball he wouldn't drop.

Seinfeld's dedication reminded me of Warren Buffet's teaching on the inner versus the outer scorecard. "The big question about how people behave is whether they've got an Inner Scorecard or an Outer Scorecard. It helps if you can be satisfied with an Inner Scorecard."[5] Your inner scorecard is how you personally define success, and no one can really answer if you have been successful but you; no one can define success for you but you. In other words, you know what game you are playing and what success looks like. This isn't the dealer's choice; you set the rules.

I struggle so much with wanting to live by an outer scorecard. *What do people think of me? Do I appear successful? Do I dress in a way that says I have my life together but also not like I am trying too hard?* You can imagine how dangerous this can get when living a life largely shared online. When I do this, I am not playing by the rules of my game but rather by the rules of someone else's. An inner scorecard takes into account what I actually think is important. It's a scorecard specific to my game.

It measures what a successful life would mean to me. When I think about my life in those terms, about what I care about and not what others see about me, it is much simpler. I want to love my family well. I want to have time for my children. I want to be easily interruptible and fun to be around. I know we also want to be in a position where it is easy to be generous when we come across someone in need. This means we cannot live to the outer edges of what we earn because we won't have any to give away.

Let's play this out. Nate and I buy a home that is outside of our budget and stretches us financially. A friend buys a house well within their budget, because it is important to them to have financial freedom. Our house is both larger and nicer than theirs. From an outer scorecard perspective, we might appear more wealthy or successful than they are. We might be able to host bigger parties or have a pool all the neighborhood kids love to swim in. However, we no longer have the financial freedom to do a lot of the things we want to do. We stress when it comes to hosting a party because of all the extra expenses that come with having people over. We hear of a need and want to help but are too stretched to do so. Our outer scorecard might look great, but we are not doing well on our inner scorecard. Likewise, our friends might live a much less glamorous life that no one is particularly impressed by, but they do not have financial stress and can give without a second thought when a need arises. Their outer scorecard might look less impressive, but their inner scorecard is soaring.

Matthew McConaughey put his own spin on this a few years ago. He had a production company, a music label, a foundation, an acting career, and a family. He explained on the *Daily Stoic* podcast, "I'm making B's in five things. I want to make A's in three things. I want to be an actor for hire, have a foundation, and be a family man."[6] In other words, he knew he was excelling on the outer scorecard, but his inner scorecard was suffering. He was making B's in areas he knew he should be making A's. He was insanely successful but not actually happy, because he knew he wasn't really living for what he knew should be most important.

Here's how I want this to look in my life: Having a welcoming home is something I really want to get an A in. Having a home that is clean and perfect is something I am fine to get a C in. I am ok when a friend comes over and sees my C-level tidiness because I live with four tiny humans. My neighbor arrives home in a brand-new Lexus. Would a new car be nice? Sure. But it's not something that ranks high on my scorecard because there are things I value more to spend my money on.

Sounds easy, right? In reality, this is really, really hard for me. I want a welcoming home that is also clean. I want to buy the Lexus and have money for the other stuff. I want to be a successful businesswoman and the ever-present mom. I want to get all A's, and it's just not possible. There are things I really want for my family and also things I want for my work, but those things can often be at odds with one another. And all the goals also come with a lot of pain and sacrifice, something we never see from Barbie. You don't see Doctor Barbie crying and stressed as she studies for the MCATs. We really don't even see Jerry Seinfeld's struggles. Much like the Instagram squares, we see the beauty of the end result, but there is a lot of sacrifice to get to the result.

I can also struggle to believe that happiness and success are limited resources, like a zero-sum game. A zero-sum game means that whatever one side gains the other side loses. By the grace of God, happiness doesn't work this way! There is enough to go around; life isn't graded on a curve. God doesn't say He only has a handful of A's to give out. My friend loving and enjoying her life does not diminish my ability to do the same. There is more than enough good to go around. Also, we might have completely different inner scorecards. The real danger comes when I get fixated on someone else's game, when I lean my ladder against a wall I never actually wanted to climb.

When I think of my own inner scorecard, I know I want to give the best of myself to Nate and the kids. I want people to feel like our home is a safe place to come and sit and be welcomed and loved. I want to be a good sister, daughter, and friend. I want what the people in my real life say about me to matter far beyond what people online say about me. I want what God says about me to have the final say. This is much harder than it appears, because something will have to give, and that something is likely the outer scorecard. This is hard because that's the card people see, and I care a lot about what people think about me.

When Barbie visits the real world, her scorecard changes. The absence of flat feet and cellulite no longer defines a happy life for her. Barbie—who from all we can see has the perfect body, the perfect career, the perfect life (the perfect outer scorecard)—wants to become human. She recognizes that there is more beyond the perfection of Barbie Land; perfection no longer defines success for her. Ruth Handler (the creator of Barbie) warns her that being a human isn't all it's cracked up to be: "You understand that humans only have one ending. . . . Being a human can be pretty uncomfortable. . . . And then you die."[7] But Barbie wants it, because she wants a whole life. The aging and the cellulite and pain are part of what make for a real, beautiful life. What will happen for Barbie? That part we don't know, but I can assume she will get wrinkles, and have hard days, and cry, and maybe post her highs on social media. She will no longer live forever, perfect in Barbie Land. She will die. But she will die having lived a real, true life. She will die, but she will have won the game that really mattered to her.

> **MINDSET SHIFT:** One of the most powerful ways to fight comparison is to define my game and what is on my inner scorecard. If I can get serious about what matters to me, I can own my choices and stop worrying about how I stack up on scorecards that aren't even mine. But first, I have to define what my game is, then fight like crazy to keep my eyes on my own priorities.

MAKING IT PRACTICAL

1. Take some time to sit down and really ask what game you're playing. What truly matters to you? What would a win look like? What things are on your inner scorecard?

2. On social media, scroll with this lens: "What is this person seeking to remember and celebrate?" The sunset. The anniversary. The trip. The picnic in the park where the baby miraculously didn't scream the whole time. It's one nanosecond of their day. A blip they could be clinging to in an otherwise difficult season. The moment I frame it that way, so much of the comparison and envy dissipates.

3. What areas of life are you wanting to get an A in? What areas would you be happy with a C, or even a D?

4. Are there habits in your life you could focus on enjoying rather than only looking to the finish line? For example: Is there an exercise you enjoy doing versus only focusing on weight loss? Or is there a new skill you want to learn that will take work, but the work could be its own form of enjoyment?

5. In his book *The Road to Character*, David Brooks talks about the difference between résumé virtues and eulogy virtues.[8] Résumé virtues are the impressive accomplishments, the things that set you apart in the job market. Eulogy virtues, on the other hand, are the things people bring up at your funeral, the things not written on paper: kindness and honesty, your character, if you were a nice person to be around, if you loved your family well. Brooks says that résumé virtues do matter, and there is likely a time in every person's life where they focus heavily on those virtues in order to build a career. But eventually, it's the eulogy virtues we all come back to. What are the eulogy virtues you want to be true of your life?

CHAPTER 10

I Just Wish That Had Gone Better

> If you think of this world as a place intended simply for our happiness, you find it quite intolerable: think of it as a place of training and correction and it's not so bad.[1]
> —C.S. Lewis, *God in the Dock*

On the enneagram scale, I am a three (the achiever/performer), but I have always identified greatly with the basic fear of a seven (the enthusiast). The enthusiast's basic fear is being deprived or in pain, and I would confess I have spent a great deal of my life seeking to avoid those two things. I hate all forms of fasting and physical discomfort. I barely wear heels, much less take on larger discomforts. I'm happy to miss out on supposed transformational experiences like cold plunging and unmedicated childbirth. I am constantly on the hunt for fun things for our family to do, often at the cost of everyone's energy (mine included) and will go to great lengths and make impressive excuses to avoid suffering of any kind. And up until this point in life, I have done a pretty great job with it. The problem with this way of living is that it really isn't very sustainable. One can only jump from one activity to another for so long, and when you are chasing down fun, disappointment is close at hand.

There are certain universal bothers that we as humans seem to unite around. Two that come up in conversation most often are weather and traffic. It's always too hot or too cold or rainy or buggy or humid. Same goes for traffic. No matter where you live or how small your town is, traffic to one degree or another exists. Nate recently told me he hopes they never find a solution to traffic because it's one of few things left that everyone can band together to complain about. Traffic and weather unite us, and I would add one more to the list: unmet expectations. Though the circumstances may all be different, everyone deals daily with things that didn't go as planned; everyone has had disappointment.

Licensed marriage and family therapist Randy Carlson says, "An expectation minus the reality of that situation will always equal disappointment.... There's only one of two things you can change, either your expectation or reality, if you don't want to have so much disappointment."[2]

I am using the word *disappointment* as opposed to tragedy very much on purpose, because I do not think I am the right person to write a chapter on tragedy. I do, however, have a lot of experience in disappointment, mostly because I am a pro at having grandiose expectations. Unfortunately, when I experience something that doesn't go as planned, my first desire is a do-over. I do not want to manage my expectations but rather try my hardest to alter the reality. When a do-over is not possible, despondency sets in. I also wanted this chapter to focus on disappointment because I feel like it is something we have all been through. Perhaps you even know someone going through a tragedy. Their pain makes you see how good you've got it, and yet you still struggle with small inconveniences and things that didn't go the way you hoped they would.

Millie was our third baby and by far the most enjoyable postpartum experience. This was the first baby I had in Charleston, so family was nearby and willing to help. Nate was working for a global law firm that offered absolutely incredible paternity leave, and it was late September in Charleston. By the time I came through those first two blurry weeks, October was here, and with it, all the promises of the heat and humidity lifting in the swamp that we called home.

There's a photo of me with Millie in a baby wrap. I am standing on tiptoes taking a photo with my nice camera over a plate of muffins. I do not remember this particular day, but looking back, all I can think is, *Wow, Kate! You felt good enough to make homemade muffins at two weeks postpartum.* I had hit the hormonal jackpot and found myself in a state of daily euphoria.

I remember one night in particular when Millie was around three weeks old when Nate and I went on a date to an outdoor shopping mall. We went into Athleta, where I purchased two pairs of pants that fit my new postpartum body, we walked around, and then we ate loads of pizza at a little Italian restaurant. Millie slept like an angel in her little bassinet while people paused at our table to ask about her, in awe that I was out and about and that we looked so comfortable as parents. We were out with one child when we really had three, I was buying pants that fit, and people were praising my parenting. As you can imagine, this was a high moment in my postpartum journey. A scene I saw myself repeating when baby number four came a few years later.

Unfortunately, things with Alberta were very different, and I could tell something was off from the moment we left the hospital. I was overly nervous to leave my comfortable room on the labor and delivery floor, even going so far as to ask the nurse as she was wheeling me out of the elevator to our car exactly how much work it would be to readmit me and get me back upstairs. Panic set in as we drove over the bridge, and I remember crying hourly that first night at home with her. No monitors constantly checking her vitals, no nurses checking in, just me and this new tiny, helpless baby. My anxiety was through the roof, and I wasn't exactly sure why. You would think by baby four I would be a pro. I would know what to do, how to nurse, how to get her to sleep, which pacifier to use. Instead I felt like a first-time mom: overwhelmed and clueless.

In those first few weeks, a dear friend (who also had four children) offered to come and bring me food. She told me she would be coming without her children, and I remember feeling so relieved. The thought of having her kids over (who were the same ages as my own and would play wonderfully with them) completely overwhelmed me. The very next day, I had a friend with three children bringing dinner, and I was in a completely different headspace; I told her to bring her kids. The thought of her family stopping by felt like something to look forward to, like something I could handle. Within the span of twenty-four hours, I went from anxious and antisocial to a welcoming hostess. This was also how I felt around outings. One moment I loved the thought of going on a family walk or to the beach, and the next I couldn't imagine leaving the house. I couldn't trust myself to make plans, because within the span of a few hours I would regret it and want to cancel them.

The weeks that came after gave me very little reprieve. Nate had started a new job that didn't offer paternity leave, so he headed back to work, and as much as people came to help, I always had this sense that I was drowning. I was exhausted and overwhelmed and on the tipping point of rage upward of ten times a day. My emotions were a series of rolling hills that I had absolutely no way of predicting. I could be cool, calm, and collected during a toddler meltdown and then ten minutes later have a meltdown of my own over a cup knocked over. Quite literally crying over spilled milk. I felt so unlike myself, so hopeless. Which in turn led to ample guilt because *Why in the world would I be sad?! I just had my fourth healthy baby! How could I be so selfish as to be sad when there are women out there hoping for one healthy baby?*

Postpartum depression and anxiety are tricky beasts, because you often don't realize you are experiencing them until they have passed. You don't know how low you are until you start to come up again. I didn't know how bad it all was until months later when I looked back and thought, *Wow, that was awful. I was not myself.*

My nursing experience with Alberta was another struggle. Prior to getting pregnant with her, I underwent a surgery called a ductectomy in order to biopsy a small area on my right breast. This area showed up on a mammogram followed by an MRI after my complaining of some pain around my right nipple. The doctor was not overly concerned but said they wanted a biopsy just to be sure. The only thing to be aware of was that this could affect my ability to nurse should we have more children. He said it was possible the ducts would compensate or even potentially repair themselves. He was hopeful, so I was hopeful. Plus, the greater need to figure out what was going on and make sure it wasn't anything serious far outweighed nursing complications for a future baby I was not even pregnant with. The procedure involved me being put under anesthesia and then having a surgeon go in and cut a small area of my milk ducts right behind the nipple. The recovery absolutely sucked, but eventually all I had was a teeny scar, and I went on with life. The biopsy came back benign (Praise God! Just some thick scar tissue likely from earlier cases of mastitis), and I didn't think much of it.

Once Alberta was born, nursing started great, but within a week I knew something wasn't working. After coming home and having my milk come in, we quickly learned my right breast (the one that had the surgery) was not working properly. Imagine a six-lane highway, but four of the lanes are closed. That was basically what was happening to the ducts in my right breast. A giant milky traffic jam. Mastitis ensued. And then, about two weeks in, my right boob just gave up. That thing was completely tuckered out. It had nursed other babies, been through surgery, and then . . . poof, it died. And so, my tried-and-true left boob took over. For the next two months, I nursed Alberta on one side. I will say, the female body really is amazing because my left side took over and got to work. However, you can imagine how this was for my overall morale. My breasts were completely different sizes. A raisin right boob and an engorged-watermelon left boob. I was so uneven in anything I tried to wear, and I went so far as to go on Amazon and buy these silicone breast enhancers in order to make them look even. These came in a two pack and were definitely being advertised for sexy twenty-year-olds to obtain optimal cleavage, but your girl stuck that rubber chicken filet in her bra every day to give her right boob a fighting chance at appearing normal.

It took about a month for me to realize this was no way to live. My left boob was working overtime, the silicone enhancers were starting to smell from the underboob sweat they were accumulating, and I was concerned my breasts would forever look completely different. Not like twins, not even like sisters, more like second cousins where one got the ugly gene. Many meltdowns later, I finally stopped nursing completely, and we switched Alberta to formula.

To be clear, I had no issue with the idea of formula. The larger disappointment was in realizing my body was not able to do what I expected of it. I had this dream of an easy baby, who I would simply nurse when she was hungry, my body perfectly performing the task needed to keep my newborn alive. Instead, I got multiple rounds of mastitis before finally surrendering to formula. Looking back, it's unfortunate that I was not better prepared for what happened with nursing. The surgeon had warned me that nursing issues could be a real outcome, and yet I still went in fully intending for everything to go perfectly. I don't know if I was too optimistic or had an overinflated view of what my body could do, but in my mind, I had failed. My body had failed. This marked the first three months of Alberta's life. Undiagnosed postpartum anxiety, mastitis, uneven breasts, and a mountain of unmet expectations.

I mourned my postpartum season with Alberta, and sometimes I still do. Partly because I so badly dreamed it would be different, and partly because it was very likely my last. I still think about how different it was—how much worse I felt—from when I had Millie, or even Scout. I was so disappointed by it that, for a long time, I toyed with us having another baby just so I could have another chance. I wanted an opportunity to alter reality; I wanted that postpartum redo. It took over two years for me to accept that postpartum experience for what it was and be ok with it. My expectations weren't met, it didn't go as planned, and I likely wasn't going to have another chance to do it over.

My sister had her own disappointments in this area. Anna is honest-to-goodness the strongest person I know. I remember back in middle school she wanted a second hole in her ear and my mom said no, so you know what Anna did? She went upstairs and shoved a needle right through her ear (I am pretty sure I dry heaved watching her do it). Anna has always had the highest tolerance for pain, and we joked at how easy childbirth would be for her. She would be one of those people to accidentally birth her child over a toilet thinking she was just having a large bowel movement. Anna was in the room for three of my four childbirths (Covid protocols being the only thing that kept her from obtaining a perfect four-for-four record), and even after having a very front-row seat to all it entailed, she remained excited to do it herself.

Anna wanted an unmedicated birth at our local birth center. She read the birthing books, ate the right foods, and was genuinely ready for the challenge. This entire plan caused our grandfather (who would sit in the waiting room during the birth of every great-grandchild) a massive amount of anxiety (he wanted all his offspring to be born in a hospital with access to all the doctors and medicine). A month before her due date, they learned the baby was breech. Anna did all the things to try to turn him and was successful in the process. Yay, back on track for the birth center! And then, the week of her due date, he flipped again, and a C-section was scheduled. Anna gave birth to her first son in a hospital with loads of medication and a large scar to tell the story. While we were all so grateful, the birth and subsequent recovery were nothing like she'd hoped.

With her second baby, she opted to try for a VBAC (vaginal birth after cesarean). She was so excited that day. Nervous, of course, but just so happy the baby wasn't breech and she could try for a vaginal birth. I was there the whole day, watching as she labored for hours and hours and never reached full dilation. She was in so much pain, which didn't seem right for someone I knew to be so strong. Something wasn't right. At 11 p.m., after laboring for twenty-five hours, the doctor on call came in to tell her they thought it was best and safest for her and the baby to do another C-section. He was stuck in the birth canal, and she wasn't dilating enough for a safe vaginal delivery. I was in the room when they told her, and my memory of seeing the disappointment and devastation on her face still brings tears to my eyes. She had labored for so long, and the end result was the same as her first. At midnight they wheeled her back, physically and emotionally exhausted, to perform surgery for a second time.

This was something Anna grappled with for months after birth, her painful abdominal scar a daily reminder of things that didn't go as planned. When talking about it later, she said it had always been her dream to go into labor and birth a baby, to do the act that would connect her to so many women in history who had gone before her. The emotion she struggled with the most was anger. Anger that showed up in the sharpest of pain around her incision every time she needed to sit up in bed or use the bathroom. Anger that whispered that her body had failed her.

In those weeks after Anna's second delivery, I remember thinking how incredible and brave she had been. Her body had not failed her. She was still stronger than any woman I have ever known. She didn't need any redo to prove how incredible she was. But I could also relate to her anger and feeling like her body had malfunctioned. We both had scars, hers on her stomach and mine on my breast, which told a tale of something in our body failing—scars to remember disappointments and grief. Like me, Anna's postpartum experience was not what she expected. Like me, she likely wouldn't get a do-over.

Our stories are just a few of thousands if not millions that end in disappointment. And truth be told, while we didn't have the experience we wanted, we both have healthy, happy babies to show for it. On the one hand, this can feel like we really shouldn't complain at all. Compared to the woman who has had a miscarriage or deals with infertility, we are lucky. Our grief is laughable, cruel even, when compared with someone who experiences a stillbirth. Our hard situations would be the best outcomes to another. Where Anna sees a scar of a failed vaginal birth, another would see a scar of a successful C-section. I have a scar on my breast, but I do not have breast cancer.

As a Christian, I know I should expect disappointment. C.S. Lewis writes this in *A Grief Observed*,

> We were even promised sufferings. They were part of the programme. We were even told, "Blessed are they that mourn," and I accepted it. I've got nothing that I hadn't bargained for. Of course it is different when the thing happens to oneself, not to others, and in reality, not imagination.[3]

It's that last line I most relate to. Suffering is not objective but rather extremely personal and subjective. Like Lewis says, "it is different when the thing happens to oneself."[4]

As someone on a journey to deeper gratitude and contentment in my life, the idea of embracing disappointment feels at odds with that journey. How do I make fun plans and be ok when they fall apart? The more I invest in something, the deeper the pain when it doesn't work out. Even now, I see my own girls playing make-believe, and one is always the mother. When I ask them what they want to be when they grow up, the occupation they choose often changes, but their response always ends with "and a mother." I see them holding their baby dolls, and I know conception and birthing a child are not things they are guaranteed. Having a healthy baby or feeling mentally stable postpartum are not things that are guaranteed. Finding love and marriage are not things that are guaranteed. Their expectations could greatly overshadow their reality.

Sometimes we find unmet expectations in the unlikeliest of places. For the Strickler kids, it was at the most magical place on earth. If you had asked our kids the one place in the entire world they wanted to visit, they would have said Disney World. They had never been and had barely even seen a photo to have a concept of the place, but that is where they wanted to go. So, after a few years, Nate and I made it happen. We gave it to them on Christmas morning with a countdown calendar to our trip. Each day, one of them would rip off the sheet, symbolizing that we were one step closer to Mickey and all the fun and excitement that would ensue. Finally, in February, we packed the car and drove the six hours to those shiny Orlando gates.

And then, on the first day in the park, the kids didn't love it. It's not to say that they hated it, but the lines were long, and the park was crowded. They would experience a three-to-four-minute fun ride after waiting an hour to get on it, only to realize they would have to wait again in order to ride it again. They were overstimulated, and after a few hours, they were asking to go back to the hotel pool. Disney World, with all its glitz and glamour, had fallen short. The most magical place on earth wasn't all that magical.

This was a hard pill for me to swallow. We had done so much planning and spent so much money. We downloaded the Disney app and paid extra for the fast pass system. There were so many details that went into this trip happening. But if I am honest, I couldn't really blame the kids. Disney also fell short of my expectations.

And then, the icing on the cake: We ended our trip with a violent stomach bug that had us packing up early to try to get home. It started with Millie puking in Mexico at Epcot, then Nate's stepdad hightailing it back to the hotel room, followed by Scout leaving her lunch on the walkway in France. Around the time I heard my father-in-law hurling (in the adjoining room) for the fifth time, I looked at Nate and said, "I think we have to get out of here. There are simply not enough toilets for us all." Telling our kids (two of whom were already actively sick) that we were going to pack up and leave the trip early was absolutely awful. Their devastation was palpable. This trip they had dreamed about and counted down for was ending early.

I remember feeling like such a failure. I had wanted this to be the perfect family trip, and instead we were packing the car to leave, shoving the clothes (and packing systems) I had prepared so diligently into random bags to get us on the road. Thirty minutes into the drive home, John Robert started to throw up, and an hour after that I got hit. I remember texting my friends in all caps, "PLEASE PRAY THAT NATE DOESN'T START THROWING UP SO THAT WE CAN GET HOME." Miraculously, we made it home, each child falling into bed with their respective puke bowl.

It would take a few days for me to realize that Disney was a life lesson my kids (and I) desperately needed. Things would not always go as planned. There would be things they hoped for that would be cut short or canceled. They would get things they looked forward to that would not meet their expectations. I started to realize my job as a parent was less about helping them have the most fun in life and more about helping them navigate all the disappointment that would come their way. I needed to teach my children to hold the same tension I was struggling to hold: to enjoy life but expect hardship.

Life is a bit like our trip to Disney World. There are a lot of shiny and entertaining parts, but it's also a bit crowded and dirty. There are things you want to do, but the lines are long. Everything has a cost, and at the end of the day it's all pretty exhausting. Even Disney World, touted as the happiest place on earth, left us wanting. You can make the best plans and pack all the right things and still have a rough trip.

When my kids are sad, all I want is to make whatever is causing the hurt go away. I want to remove the pain, to get them back to a place of happiness. When they were younger, this was pretty easy. Most issues could be solved with a stuffed animal or sippy cup of milk. Unfortunately, as they have gotten older, I am realizing the things that bring disappointment are outside of my control. Getting cut from the basketball team or being bullied at school are not things I have a quick solution for. They are still young but are already learning the harsh reality that life is not always easy.

But how do I teach them to love life and at the same time expect disappointment? To be excited for Disney, but also to bring puke bags, just in case. How do all of us practically live in a world that is deeply fallen without becoming total cynics?

I wish I had a good answer to give, but to be totally honest, I am not sure. The best way I have found personally to deal with disappointments has been to bring them to Jesus and realize He has experienced the same. Jesus walked on the earth and knows what it feels like to have people not like you or to have an experience not go as you planned. When I remember I am living in a world that is not what God wanted it to be, I can view my role as someone seeking to help make it better instead of someone seeking to get every ounce of joy out of it. When I remember that my time on earth is small in view of eternity, the disappointments feel much more bearable. I have also found that when I personally experience disappointments, it makes me much more sympathetic to others going through a hard time.

No time was that truer than with Alberta's sleep.

If there's one thing I love, it's sleep. Put me in bed before 9 p.m., and I will practically squeal as I get under the covers. I don't sleep in, but I love going to bed early and waking up refreshed. To me, there's no better feeling than a 6 a.m. wake-up after a full nine hours. I think most any mom would say one of her top three desires is a full night's sleep. This should come as no surprise, because if there's anything that steals your sleep, it's kids. Now that I have kids, I understand why the military uses sleep deprivation as a torture tactic.

Our first three children were pretty amazing sleepers. We sleep trained John Robert just like the Babywise book told us to, no matter how neurotic the process made me, and he, living up to the obedient firstborn that he is, slowly but surely gave in to his mother's strict scheduling. Eat, wake, sleep. Eat, wake, sleep. Like a good little soldier.

Scout was nicknamed "the best baby ever" because, honestly, she was. So easy! She slept anywhere, napped anywhere. Put her in the carrier or the crib. Leave the lights on or turn them off. She made having two kids feel easy, because she was so easy. Millie was a second Scout. The only difference was that she actually slept longer than her sister! We joked that Millie didn't drop her morning nap, she absorbed it, sleeping most days from 7 p.m. till 10 a.m. If we had a morning activity, I would literally have to wake Millie from her fifteen-hour slumber to get there. It was amazing.

At this point, as you can imagine, I thought I was the absolute best mom ever. My kids slept. They went down as expected. Napped as expected. They didn't rely on weak crutches like a pacifier. They performed well because I, as their incredible mother, trained them to do so.

Then came Alberta. That sweet fourth child, who had already wrecked my postpartum dreams, humbled me to my knees yet again. From day one she was fussier than her siblings, leaving me clueless as to what to do. I was so tired. I cried daily. None of the golden wisdom I had from my first three seemed to work on this stubborn fourth child. We used the sound machine, made the room dark, and used pacifiers. She simply did not want to sleep when I wanted her to sleep.

Before Alberta, I think I secretly judged people who needed help getting their baby to sleep. It's not that I didn't think they were trying but more so that they must not be trying the *right* things. If they did the things I did, their baby would sleep. Then, the things I always did, the tricks I prided myself on, couldn't get my own baby to sleep. Most days I was on the couch sobbing, fussy baby in hand, sleep-deprived and desperate. I needed help. I reached out to my friend Abby, who had built a career on helping moms get their babies to sleep, to troubleshoot what to do.

Having to ask for help to get my child to sleep was one of the most humbling things I have had to do as a young mom. Like I said, I considered myself a pro. Alberta not responding to the methods that worked for the others made me feel like maybe I wasn't all that good at motherhood, and this dip in confidence bled into other areas of my parenting. I would see a mom with her baby happily in the wrap, while Alberta screamed every time I put her in it, or a mom out at a loud coffee shop with her baby napping in the stroller, when I could scarcely get Alberta to nap in a dark room with a sound machine. I had already failed at nursing, and now I couldn't even get my baby to sleep. It absolutely sucked, and it ate at the very core of my ability as a parent. Now, a few years removed, I can see how it was an area where God was actually being very kind to me.

What I realized in the process was the pride I had in my own ability was replaced with something much softer. Something more welcoming and easier to hold: humility. Humility is the opposite of pride. When you are hung up on pride, you can't experience the freedom humility offers. Humility allows you to realize you don't have all the answers and frees you to ask someone for help.

Something else I came to realize was how much my pride was keeping me from empathy. When you think you're awesome, it's hard to see someone struggling and empathize with them. The moment I realized I didn't actually have the ability to get my baby to sleep, I all of a sudden felt a deep sense of understanding for others in the same boat. The thought *They just aren't doing the right things* was replaced with *I bet they are trying everything they can think of and it's just not working*. I could identify with their disappointment.

My own disappointments led me to a softness for others I might not have had if Alberta was a great sleeper. You can empathize with the mom in the grocery store with the screaming child when you yourself have dealt with tantrums. You can relate to someone struggling with depression when you yourself have felt its hopeless grasp. Humility softens us. It is like a warm blanket, ready to wrap around someone who needs to be understood.

As much as I want to shield myself from disappointment, and as much as I want to protect my kids from it, I now know that it can be a universal softener. Suffering, even the smallest of kinds like traffic and a child's sleep, can be a glue to unite us all. It's a gentle nudge to loosen the expectations I have of this life being perfect and happy, and to be kind, knowing others are going through the same. When I allow life to have its disappointments, my delight is all the greater when things go well. Paradoxically, the disappointments can allow my gratitude in life to increase and my empathy for others to grow as well.

> **MINDSET SHIFT:** Welcoming suffering not only deepens my gratitude for when things are going well, but it also softens me to empathize with and be kind to others, knowing they are likely going through hardship of their own.

・・・・・・ MAKING IT PRACTICAL ・・・・・・

1. Reread the opening quote by C.S. Lewis. What areas of your life feel hard but could actually be an opportunity for training and correction?

2. Take on a redemptive worldview: When we see our lives as part of a greater mission to make the world better, we look to add good to it but aren't surprised when things go badly. Is there an area where you have felt disappointment that you could help another feel more joy? For me, I want to always have my eyes open to other moms in a tough postpartum season. Perhaps in helping them, I get the added benefit of healing my own postpartum wounds. Is there someone in a tough season that you could make better?

3. If you are in a hard season, have you let people in your life in on it? Can you think of one tangible way you could ask a friend to help you?

4. If you are in a thriving season, are there a few people you could offer to help in some way? Think of one tangible, specific action step (ex: bringing a meal, doing a carpool pickup, grabbing a load of laundry to wash and return), and text a friend to offer that to her this week.

5. Allow disappointments you face as a family to be teaching moments for your children. This is a really helpful way to model managing expectations and has so many life applications for when anything, big or small, does not go as planned. Truthfully, I did not do this well at all after our Disney World puke fest, but I would bet good money I will have another opportunity in the near future.

CHAPTER 11

A Life You Love

The Skin Horse had lived longer in the nursery than any of the others. He was so old that his brown coat was bald in patches and showed the seams underneath, and most of the hairs in his tail had been pulled out to string bead necklaces. He was wise, for he had seen a long succession of mechanical toys arrive to boast and swagger, and by-and-by break their mainsprings and pass away, and he knew that they were only toys, and would never turn into anything else. For nursery magic is very strange and wonderful, and only those playthings that are old and wise and experienced like the Skin Horse understand all about it. . . .

"Real isn't how you are made," said the Skin Horse. "It's a thing that happens to you. When a child loves you for a long, long time, not just to play with, but REALLY loves you, then you become Real."

"Does it hurt?" asked the Rabbit.

"Sometimes," said the Skin Horse, for he was always truthful. "When you are Real you don't mind being hurt."

"Does it happen all at once, like being wound up," he asked, "or bit by bit?"

> "It doesn't happen all at once," said the Skin Horse. "You become. It takes a long time. That's why it doesn't happen often to people who break easily, or have sharp edges, or who have to be carefully kept. Generally, by the time you are Real, most of your hair has been loved off, and your eyes drop out and you get loose in the joints and very shabby. But these things don't matter at all, because once you are Real you can't be ugly, except to people who don't understand."
>
> —Margery Williams, *The Velveteen Rabbit*

A few years back, I was looking for a specific photo of Scout when I had an epiphany of sorts. I was scrolling through photo after photo on my phone from the season of life when we were living in a rental house with outdated appliances and a bathroom completely tiled in yellow.

I pulled out a photo of a toddler-aged John Robert, beaming from ear to ear with a pile of bubbles on his head and that butter-colored tile in the background. There was another one of me, nine months pregnant, lounging in that same bathroom sipping a green smoothie in a bubble bath. I can remember the house only had one tub, and I would take out all the toddler toys nightly in order to soak my aching back. We brought Scout home to that house, and there's a million photos of her napping with Nate on the old brown couch our friends passed down to us (yes, the one with the duct taped back from falling out of the pickup truck). There were photos of meals I cooked on the old electric stovetop with the unreliable oven, friends crowded around the dining room table with the mismatched chairs.

As I flipped through photo after photo, what I noticed more than anything was the people. I am sure in those old houses I just wished for countertops that weren't Formica or a bathroom of my own. But in hindsight, those details fade away. What is left are the people and the memories, the richness of each season. These photos offered me a clear moment of hindsight. When I think about my life as a series of photos, I wonder what will matter most to me. Who I want to be with in them, where we are, what we are doing. I pray that what I look like or what I am wearing or what car I am driving will hold little weight compared to the people in the photos.

When I first gave the title for this book, the subtitle read "And Other Lies I *Thought* Would Make Me Happy." It was only after finishing that I went back and changed it to the present tense. As I wrote, I realized that so much said here is a working narrative in my brain, ideas and ideals I marinate on often but have not yet mastered.

It's a funny dichotomy to write a book on the subject of loving your life. To some degree, I feel like a fraud. I'm thirty-five years old and am still struggling with so much of what I wrote about. Perhaps there is something to be said of being in the thick of it as I write. Time has not had the ability to color my experience in a guise of wisdom. I am still working through what game I am playing; I am still fighting not to catch my reflection too long in the mirror or feel shame for my body as it ages; I am still grappling with how to spend both my money and my days.

When I started this book, I saw the practical steps as something I could do alongside God, with Him as the resting place for when the practical failed me. But as I have written, I have come to realize God is much more hands-on than I give Him credit for. He cares about the details I consider trite. Sometimes my head is in a bad place and I'm wishing for a bigger kitchen, and sometimes I actually just need to wipe my counters and load the dishwasher. Both can be true. Where I saw the pragmatic steps as being outside of faith, they are actually the nooks and crannies He provides. My practicality is not outside of who He is but rather crucial to my ability to climb and hold on. But it gets better: As a Christian, the promise of Christ sets me apart from the risk of a free fall Alex Honnold faced as he climbed El Capitan. When I slip and my entire body hangs suspended over the rocks down below, God is the rope that catches me. When I lose hope, Christ is the harness that holds me. I can lean back, take a breath, wipe the sweat, and begin climbing again. His understanding and patience know no bounds.

I hope this book has brought some clarity and freedom to your own "I just wish..." thoughts. I hope that the more you look for all the ways things work for good outside of your control, the more you are able to let go of control. Whether you are thirty-five or sixty-five, there is so much joy and goodness here for you now, and you don't need to fret over past days spent just wishing. Abundant grace abounds both now and on the days you find yourself struggling (because we all have those days). More than anything, I feel grateful to have gotten the opportunity to write, because it has forced me to sit down and reflect on what matters to me. While not perfect, I do feel much more clear on whose game I am playing and whose I am not. I feel more confident in the friendships that I have, more decided on what I want my children to see when they look at my life and my values. I hold my inner scorecard close to the chest.

This is our one life, and we have more power than we realize for how much we can enjoy it. If a certain chapter resonated with you, I hope you go back and work through the practical steps and questions at the end. Maybe you need to turn the mirror around for a month, or take a social media break, or get a date on the calendar for coffee with a trusted friend. The small shifts in how you go about your life hold weight. The habits and routines you create act as guardrails, keeping your eyes on what matters. And as you live into that life—your specific life, the one precious life you have been given—you find a contentment blossoming. You can abandon the online shopping cart when you realize you are so much more than the clothes you wear. You can love your husband better when you remember he is a whole person with struggles and strengths just like you have. You can be happy for your friends' victories, knowing happiness is not a zero-sum game.

My friend Caitlin shared the opening quote for this chapter with me as I was writing this book. Essentially, the Skin Horse explains to the Velveteen Rabbit what it means to become real. Becoming real happens when you are loved for a very long time. It's a slow process that isn't for the faint of heart. You can't be too delicate; sometimes it hurts and leaves marks on you. The Skin Horse is worn, with bald patches and missing hair, but he doesn't care, "because once you are Real you can't be ugly, except to people who don't understand."[1]

I want a life like the Skin Horse's. A life that is real because it is loved. A beat-up, well-lived, beautiful life that comes more alive as I love it. A life so real it can't possibly be ugly.

Don't get me wrong, this is hard work. I used the mountain climbing metaphor for a reason. But it is good, worthy work. A work that brings deep satisfaction in the effort. And I believe wholeheartedly that with each day, with each moment you grab hold and cling to where God has you and what matters most in your own life, your grip strength will increase. You'll learn the areas that feel hardest to climb and get better at the practical ways to work through them. And eventually, you will look way down and see all those days of just wishing, but they will feel like a distant memory. You'll take stock of how far you've climbed, find a place to rest, and enjoy the glorious view of the life right in front of you.

Notes

Introduction

1. In 1914, Dr. Frank Crane wrote an article for the *Syracuse Herald*. In it, he wrote this quote, crediting Abraham Lincoln with saying it. It's never been verified by any other sources.

Chapter 1 I Just Wish I Had a Bigger Kitchen

1. Myquillyn Smith, *Cozy Minimalist Home: More Style, Less Stuff* (Zondervan, 2018), 80.

Chapter 2 I Just Wish I Was a Better Mom

1. Dr. Becky Kennedy, PhD (@drbeckyatgoodinside), Instagram, June 4, 2023, https://www.instagram.com/reel/CtFXvS5ACSm/?utm_source=ig_web_copy_link&igsh=MzRlODBiNWFlZA==.

Chapter 3 I Just Wish I Had a Better Husband

1. *Good Will Hunting*, directed by Gus Van Sant, written by Matt Damon and Ben Affleck, (1997; Miramax, 1998), DVD.
2. *Good Will Hunting*, Van Sant, DVD.
3. Timothy Keller with Kathy Keller, *The Meaning of Marriage: Facing the Complexities of Commitment with the Wisdom of God* (Penguin Books, 2011), 101.
4. Keller with Keller, *The Meaning of Marriage*, 44.
5. "Define romance," Google Search, accessed July 17, 2024, https://www.google.com/search?q=define+romance.
6. C.S. Lewis, *The Four Loves* (Harcourt Brace Jovanovich, 1991), 65. *The Four Loves* by C.S. Lewis copyright ©1960 C.S. Lewis Pte. Ltd. Extract reprinted by permission.
7. C.S. Lewis, *The Four Loves* (Harcourt Brace Jovanovich, 1991), 65. *The Four Loves* by C.S. Lewis copyright ©1960 C.S. Lewis Pte. Ltd. Extract reprinted by permission.

8. C.S. Lewis, *The Four Loves* (Harcourt Brace Jovanovich, 1991), 65. *The Four Loves* by C.S. Lewis copyright ©1960 C.S. Lewis Pte. Ltd. Extract reprinted by permission.

Chapter 4 I Just Wish I Had More Friends

1. Shauna Niequist, *Bittersweet: Thoughts on Change, Grace, and Learning the Hard Way* (Zondervan, 2010), 79.

Chapter 5 I Just Wish I Looked Better

1. Rick Warren, *The Purpose Driven Life: What on Earth Am I Here For?*, expanded ed. (Zondervan, 2012), 149.

2. "Define vain," Google Search, accessed July 15, 2024, https://www.google.com/search?q=define+vain.

3. *Friends*, season 4, episode 4, "The One with the Ballroom Dancing," written by David Crane, Marta Kauffman, Andrew Reich, and Ted Cohen, directed by Gail Mancuso, aired October 16, 1997.

4. Jane Fonda, "Julia Gets Wise with Jane Fonda," interview by Julia Louis-Dreyfus, *Wiser Than Me*, audio podcast, April 11, 2023, https://open.spotify.com/episode/3Lhq0WfFyOGa1O5w8MxRzb.

5. Sally Field, "Julia Gets Wise with Sally Field," interview by Julia Louis-Dreyfus, *Wiser Than Me*, audio podcast, March 27, 2024, https://open.spotify.com/episode/1tY1EmZmXCUhYjqwCy7ECo.

Chapter 6 I Just Wish I Had More Money

1. Nassim Nicholas Taleb, *Fooled by Randomness: The Hidden Role of Chance in Life and in the Markets*, 2nd ed. (Random House, 2004), 139–43.

2. "A Great Help to Pa," *Keeping up with the Joneses*, illustrated by Arthur Ragland "Pop" Momand (Cupples & Leon Co., 1920), https://archive.org/details/bub_gb_6QoNAAAAYAAJ/page/n19/mode/2up?q=great+help.

3. Morgan Housel, *The Psychology of Money: Timeless Lessons on Wealth, Greed, and Happiness* (Harriman House, 2020), 106.

4. Housel, *The Psychology of Money*, 41.

5. Shauna Niequist, *Savor: Living Abundantly Where You Are, As You Are* (Zondervan, 2015), 15.

Chapter 7 I Just Wish I Had More Time

1. Annie Dillard, *The Writing Life* (Harper Perennial, 2013), 32.

2. Mary Oliver, "The Summer Day," in *New and Selected Poems, Volume One* (Beacon Press, 1992), 94. "The Summer Day" by Mary Oliver reprinted by the permission of The Charlotte Sheedy Literary Agency as agent for the author. Copyright © 1990, 2006, 2008, 2017 by Mary Oliver with permission of Bill Reichblum.

3. Peter F. Drucker, "Managing for Business Effectiveness," *Harvard Business Review*, May 1963, https://hbr.org/1963/05/managing-for-business-effectiveness.

Notes

Chapter 8 I Just Wish I Had Control

1. *National Lampoon's Van Wilder*, directed by Walt Becker, written by Brent Goldberg and David Wagner (Artisan Entertainment, 2002), DVD.
2. Annie Duke, "Episode 885," interview by Steve Pomeranz, *Steve Pomeranz Show*, audio podcast, August 15, 2018, https://stevepomeranz.com/full-show/episode-885/#1491939506885-c75ae4b7-d2777ebb-168340a9-b26649df-bc25.

Chapter 9 I Just Wish My Life Looked More Like Hers

1. *Barbie*, directed by Greta Gerwig, written by Greta Gerwig and Noah Baumbach (Warner Bros. Pictures, 2023), DVD.
2. *Barbie*, Gerwig, DVD.
3. *Barbie*, Gerwig, DVD.
4. James Clear, "#348—Why Habits Don't Demand Perfection with James Clear," interview by Kendra Adachi *The Lazy Genius*, audio podcast, January 8, 2024, https://www.thelazygeniuscollective.com/lazy/jamesclear.
5. Warren Buffet as told to Alice Schroeder, *The Snowball: Warren Buffet and the Business of Life* (Bloomsbury Publishing, 2008), 32.
6. Mathew McConaughey, "Mathew McConaughey On Winning the Role of Life," interview by Ryan Holiday, *The Daily Stoic*, audio podcast, November 14, 2020, https://dailystoic.com/mcconaughey/.
7. *Barbie*, Gerwig, DVD.
8. David Brooks, *The Road to Character* (Random House, 2015), xi.

Chapter 10 I Just Wish That Had Gone Better

1. C.S. Lewis, *God in the Dock* (William B. Eerdmans Publishing Company, 1970), 52. *God in the Dock* by C.S. Lewis copyright ©1970 C.S. Lewis Pte. Ltd. Extract reprinted by permission.
2. Randy Carlson, host, *Intentional Living*, audio podcast, "Managing Your Expectations," Intentional Life Media, April 16, 2024, https://theintentionallife.com/broadcasts/managing-your-expectations/.
3. C.S. Lewis, *A Grief Observed* (United Kingdom: HarperCollins, 2001), 36–37. *A Grief Observed* by C.S. Lewis copyright ©1961 C.S. Lewis Pte. Ltd. Extract reprinted by permission.
4. C.S. Lewis, *A Grief Observed* (United Kingdom: HarperCollins, 2001), 36–37. *A Grief Observed* by C.S. Lewis copyright ©1961 C.S. Lewis Pte. Ltd. Extract reprinted by permission.

Chapter 11 A Life You Love

1. Margery Williams, *The Velveteen Rabbit: Or How Toys Become Real* (1922; reis., Doubleday, 1991), 8.

Acknowledgments

1. Anne Lamott, *Bird by Bird: Some Instructions on Writing and Life* (Anchor Books, 1995), 19.

Acknowledgments

When I started writing this book, I knew it would be a large undertaking, but I don't think I realized just how much the people around me would come to serve as a life raft when I felt like I was drowning.

Thank you to Jen, my editor, and Andy who flew down to Charleston the day before a hurricane and sat with me until I felt like the book had solid direction. From our very first meeting, Jen said she would not leave me to flounder, and she has kept true to her word. Jen, thank you for every bit of encouragement, and for pushing me to go deeper. Thank you to Lisa, my book agent, who also pushed me to write a "words book." You knew deep down I wanted to but was scared to, and you wouldn't let me settle. This book exists because of those early meetings of you convincing me that what I had to say matters.

To my early readers: John Mark, Caitlin, Kamri, Molly, and Lisa. Thank you for taking the time (and printer ink!) to read the early versions. Your thoughts and comments changed this book for the better.

Thank you so much to John and Debbie at the Jasper office building. The cubicle I sat in to write most of this book feels sacred to me. I owe you well over $1,000 in all the free coffee I drank.

Acknowledgments

It may sound silly to go this far back, but I owe so much of how I write to my English teachers. Doctor Maynard, thank you for the way you taught me to use words, for the way you pounded out the word *alliteration*, hitting every consonant, and sang *assonance*, touching on every vowel. You never settled for easy literature, having us read Whitman and perform Shakespeare. Mrs. Barrett and Mrs. Horton, I am sure I write the way I do because of your shrewd eyes, giving me a deep love for the English language and how to use it well.

I would like to thank the public school system for the countless hours you had my children, giving me time and space to write. Teachers, there are not enough words to express my gratitude for you.

To Kendra, who answered so many of my book-writing questions and made me feel normal when I wanted to burn it all down.

To Jess, without whom I would have been crushed under the weight of all the logistics of running an online business. Jess, you keep me afloat and cheer me on daily; I don't know how I got so lucky to have you on the NTK team.

To my incredible, absolutely huge "everyone is a cousin" family. Thank you for being my very first followers online—my first cheerleaders. You are the world's greatest village.

Mom, you have never wavered in believing I could do anything I set my mind to. I am sure I would have given up on Naptime Kitchen one hundred times by now if not for your encouragement and faith in me. So much of who I am and what I show people online is from you; you're the real hero. Thank you for letting me take all of your credit. Poppa, thank you for asking to get business cards made so you could hand them out to your friends to follow me online; you have never left my corner. Thank you both for the way you have shown me how to love and how to be loved. If Nate and I have a marriage like yours I will consider us deeply blessed.

To "The Ninnies": Molly, Megan, Lisa, Lindsey, Maggie, and McKenzie. I would be utterly lost without you. Thank you for being the

Acknowledgments

very best of friends I could ask for, for reading early chapters, and for loving me for exactly who I am. Y'all are the safest of havens, and every moment I get with you is never enough time. Also, thank you for making me laugh. I take motherhood and life in general much lighter because of you. After all, "if you don't laugh, you'll cry."

To everyone who has followed along with Naptime Kitchen these last nine years: I get to do this because of you. I have said it a thousand times, but I truly believe that I have the most kind and encouraging community on the internet. Thank you for every message, comment, and email. I cherish them.

To John Robert, Scout, Millie, and Allie. You four and your dad are my entire world. So much of the decision to write this book came from a desire to have something tangible you could read when you are older. I pray so much that you live lives of deep contentment, knowing who you are and Whose you are. Please know, I could never "just wish" for anything greater than the four of you. You are my greatest treasure this side of heaven and bring me more joy than I ever imagined.

Nate, I do not know where to begin. We jokingly called you my "first editor," but it's exactly what you were. You have read every single chapter in its ugliest form, and you have such a gift for taking my scattered thoughts and helping come up with a cohesive way to express them. Thank you for every single quote you pulled from memory, and for all the articles and books you pointed me to; you have made this book infinitely better. Thank you for rubbing my back during my countless meltdowns and reminding me it would get done "bird by bird."[1] Thank you for all the extra slack you picked up around the house. Dishes got done and book bags packed for school because you made it happen. Thank you for the countless bowls of scrambled eggs you would quietly set on my desk when I was deep in the zone typing. You are the greatest partner I could ever dream of spending my life with, and I promise to read your first drafts when you decide to write something of your own.

KATE STRICKLER is the creator behind the blog and Instagram account *Naptime Kitchen*, where since 2016 she has had the privilege of connecting with thousands of women across the globe. From home to the kitchen to parenting, Kate loves functionality and systems, and she knows they work best when mixed with a hefty dose of perspective and grace. When she isn't wrangling the kids or working, you can find her in her happy place: experimenting in the kitchen. Kate lives in Charleston, South Carolina, with her husband, Nate, and their four children.

· · · · · · · · · **CONNECT WITH KATE** · · · · · · · · ·

NaptimeKitchen.com

@NaptimeKitchen   @NaptimeKitchen3026